Assembly Programming for Beginners

Master the Low Level and Control Hardware from Scratch

Louis Madson

DISCOVER OTHER BOOKS IN THE SERIES..........................4

DISCLAIMER 6

INTRODUCTION 7

CHAPTER 1: INTRODUCTION TO ASSEMBLY LANGUAGE .9

UNDERSTANDING LOW-LEVEL PROGRAMMING AND ITS IMPORTANCE...13
ASSEMBLY LANGUAGE AND ITS ROLE IN MODERN COMPUTING................16

CHAPTER 2: SETTING UP YOUR ASSEMBLY
DEVELOPMENT ENVIRONMENT 21

CHOOSING AN ASSEMBLER: NASM, MASM, GAS, AND OTHERS............26
INSTALLING AND CONFIGURING YOUR FIRST ASSEMBLY PROGRAMMING
SETUP 30

CHAPTER 3: UNDERSTANDING THE CPU AND REGISTERS
.... 36

CPU ARCHITECTURE AND HOW ASSEMBLY INTERACTS WITH HARDWARE
....40
WORKING WITH REGISTERS: GENERAL-PURPOSE, SPECIAL-PURPOSE,
AND SEGMENT REGISTERS..45

CHAPTER 4: ASSEMBLY LANGUAGE SYNTAX AND
STRUCTURE...50

WRITING YOUR FIRST ASSEMBLY PROGRAM: STRUCTURE AND
COMPONENTS..54
DIRECTIVES, LABELS, AND COMMENTS: ORGANIZING YOUR CODE.........59

CHAPTER 5: MEMORY MANAGEMENT IN ASSEMBLY 65

UNDERSTANDING RAM, STACK, AND HEAP IN LOW- LEVEL
PROGRAMMING..68
ADDRESSING MODES AND HOW DATA IS ACCESSED IN MEMORY...........73

CHAPTER 6: WORKING WITH ARITHMETIC AND
LOGICAL OPERATIONS...78

PERFORMING BASIC ARITHMETIC: ADDITION, SUBTRACTION,
MULTIPLICATION, AND DIVISION..82
LOGICAL OPERATIONS AND BITWISE MANIPULATION..............................87

2

CHAPTER 7: CONTROL FLOW AND DECISION MAKING.. 93

IMPLEMENTING CONDITIONAL STATEMENTS: JUMPS AND COMPARISONS
....98
LOOPS IN ASSEMBLY: LOOP, JMP, AND CONDITIONAL BRANCHING..... 102

CHAPTER 8: WORKING WITH FUNCTIONS AND PROCEDURES.. 107

CALLING AND DEFINING PROCEDURES IN ASSEMBLY............................. 112
USING THE STACK FOR FUNCTION CALLS AND PARAMETER PASSING... 117

CHAPTER 9: HANDLING INPUT AND OUTPUT IN ASSEMBLY 122

WORKING WITH KEYBOARD INPUT AND SCREEN OUTPUT...................... 126
INTERACTING WITH SYSTEM CALLS AND BIOS INTERRUPTS 131

CHAPTER 10: UNDERSTANDING AND IMPLEMENTING INTERRUPTS 136

SOFTWARE VS. HARDWARE INTERRUPTS AND THEIR USES.................... 141
USING INTERRUPTS FOR SYSTEM-LEVEL OPERATIONS 146

CHAPTER 11: ASSEMBLY LANGUAGE AND FILE HANDLING 151

READING AND WRITING FILES IN ASSEMBLY 155
READING FROM A FILE... 157

CHAPTER 12: DEBUGGING AND TROUBLESHOOTING ASSEMBLY CODE.. 162

USING DEBUGGING TOOLS LIKE GDB AND OLLYDBG............................ 166
COMMON ASSEMBLY ERRORS AND HOW TO FIX THEM......................... 171

CONCLUSION 174

BIOGRAPHY 176

GLOSSARY: ASSEMBLY PROGRAMMING FOR BEGINNERS 176

3

Discover other books in the series

"Assembly Programming for Cyber Security: Unleash the Power of Low-Level Code to Break and Defend Systems"

"Assembly Programming for Computer Architecture: Understanding the Hardware"

"Assembly Programming for Malware Analysis: Malicious Software Development and Malware Analysis with Assembly"

"Assembly Programming for Network: Development of Communication Protocols"

"Assembly Programming for Operating Systems: Build Your Own OS from Scratch"

Disclaimer

The information provided in *"Assembly Programming for Beginners: Master the Low Level and Control Hardware from Scratch"* by Louis Madson is for educational and informational purposes only.

This Book is designed to introduce readers to the fundamentals of assembly programming and low-level hardware control. The author and publisher make no representations or warranties regarding the accuracy, completeness, or applicability of the content.

Introduction

Welcome to **"Assembly Programming for Beginners: Master the Low Level and Control Hardware from Scratch"**. In a landscape where higher-level languages dominate the software development arena, the power and elegance of assembly language often remain shrouded in mystery. This book aims to demystify that enterprise, guiding curious minds through the fundamentals of assembly programming and equipping you with the skills to interact directly with hardware.

Assembly language is the bridge between high-level programming and the raw machine code that powers your devices. Understanding it sets the stage for deeper knowledge of computer architecture, operating systems, and even the underlying principles that govern higher-level languages. Whether you're an aspiring programmer, an enthusiastic hobbyist, or a seasoned engineer seeking to enhance your skill set, this book is tailored for you.

Throughout these pages, we will explore the foundational concepts of assembly programming, breaking down complex ideas into digestible segments. You will learn about key components such as registers, memory management, and instruction sets. We will also dive into practical applications, showing you how to write, debug, and optimize assembly code. With clear explanations, hands-on examples, and exercises designed to reinforce your understanding, you will gain the confidence to manipulate hardware at a level that few ever venture to explore.

As we navigate this intricate world, you'll discover that

mastery of assembly programming is not just about syntax or theory; it's about fostering a mindset that embraces the underlying mechanics of computing. The skills you acquire will open doors to a broader understanding of software development, hardware interactions, and the performance optimizations that can be achieved through lower-level programming.

By the end of this journey, you will not only possess the knowledge to write assembly code but also appreciate the profound beauty and capability that comes from engaging with your computer at such a fundamental level. Let's take the first step together into the exciting realm of assembly programming, where every line of code you write brings you one step closer to mastering the art of controlling hardware from the ground up.

Get ready to unlock the secrets of low-level programming and embark on an adventure that could redefine your approach to technology.

Chapter 1: Introduction to Assembly Language

Assembly language differs significantly from high-level programming languages such as Python, Java, or C++, which prioritize human readability and ease of writing. Instead, assembly language offers a symbolic representation of a computer's machine code, effectively bridging the divide between human reasoning and machine instructions.

Fundamentally, assembly language comprises instructions that directly correspond to machine code operations, with each assembly instruction typically representing a singular machine action. This close relationship enables programmers to create more efficient and optimized code, as it aligns closely with the hardware's capabilities.

1.2 History of Assembly Language

The origins of assembly language can be traced back to the formative years of computing in the 1940s and 1950s. During this era, programmers were required to write code in binary, a process that was both laborious and prone to errors. To alleviate these challenges, early computer scientists developed symbolic representations of machine code, which led to the establishment of assembly languages.

The initial assembly languages were crafted for specific types of hardware, and as computer architectures advanced, assembly languages evolved accordingly. Each assembly language was specifically designed to leverage the unique characteristics of its corresponding hardware. For instance, x86 assembly language is utilized for Intel and AMD processors, while ARM assembly language is employed for ARM processors commonly found in smartphones and tablets.## 1.3 Characteristics of Assembly Language

Assembly language has several distinct characteristics that set it apart from higher-level languages:

Low-Level Nature: Assembly language operates at a low level, meaning it provides direct control over hardware resources such as registers, memory, and input/output operations.

Hardware Specificity: Each assembly language is specific to a particular computer architecture. Programs written in assembly for one architecture cannot run on another without modifications.

Efficiency: Assembly language allows programmers to write highly efficient code, as it permits fine- tuned manipulation of hardware resources, enabling optimization for speed and size.

Lack of Abstraction: Assembly language lacks many of the abstractions found in high-level languages. Concepts like classes, objects, and built-in functions are not present, and programmers must manage resources directly.

Mnemonics: Assembly language uses human-readable mnemonics instead of binary code. For example, the mnemonic `MOV` might be used to represent the operation of moving data from one place to another, making it easier for programmers to read and understand the code.

1.4 Basic Structure of Assembly Language Programs

An assembly language program consists of a series of

instructions that the CPU can execute. Each instruction is generally comprised of an operation code (opcode) and operands that specify the data to be manipulated. A simple assembly program may look as follows:

```assembly
section .data ; Data segment message db 'Hello, World!',0
; String to print

section .text ; Code segment

global _start ; Entry point for the program

_start:

mov rax, 1     ; syscall number for sys_write

mov rdi, 1     ; file descriptor for stdout mov rsi, message
                    ; address of string to print mov rdx, 13
               ; length of the string

syscall; make the system call to print

mov rax, 60   ; syscall number for sys_exit

xor rdi, rdi    ; exit code 0

syscall; make the system call to exit
```

In this example, the program initializes a string in the data section and then writes that string to standard output before exiting. Each line demonstrates typical instructions used in assembly language, reflecting its operational nature.

1.5 Importance of Assembly Language

Though higher-level languages have dominated modern

programming due to their ease of use and abstraction from hardware, assembly language remains crucial for several reasons:

Performance Tuning: Critical sections of performance-critical applications (such as operating systems, embedded systems, and game engines) may be optimized using assembly.

System Level Programming: Assembly language provides direct access to hardware resources, making it indispensable for system-level programming like device drivers and firmware development.

Learning Tool: Understanding assembly language helps programmers gain deeper insights into how computers work, enabling them to write better, more efficient code in high-level languages.

Assembly language is a powerful tool that, while less commonly used for general application development, offers invaluable insights and control for systems programming and performance optimization. As the backbone of any software that runs on hardware, mastering assembly language can greatly enhance a programmer's skill set and understanding of computer architecture.

Understanding Low-Level Programming and Its Importance

In an era where high-level programming languages dominate the development landscape, the significance of low-level programming often gets overshadowed. However, low-level programming holds a crucial position in the realm of computer science and software development. This chapter aims to shed light on what low-level programming entails, its unique characteristics, and why it remains an important facet of technology today.

What is Low-Level Programming?

Low-level programming refers to coding that is closely related to the machine's hardware. It typically involves programming languages that provide little to no abstraction from a computer's instruction set architecture. The most notable examples of low-level programming languages include Assembly language and machine code.

Characteristics of Low-Level Programming

Close to Hardware: Low-level programming offers direct control over hardware components, allowing programmers to manipulate memory addresses and CPU registers.

Performance and Efficiency: Since it operates close to the machine level, low-level programming can produce highly efficient machine code, leading to fast execution and minimal resource consumption.

Hardware-Specific: Low-level code is often hardware-dependent, meaning that programs written in this style may not run on different architectures without significant modification.

Limited Abstraction: Unlike high-level languages, low-level programming provides less abstraction, which can lead to more complex and less intuitive code.

The Role of Low-Level Programming in Software Development

While high-level languages like Python, Java, and C# are favored for their user-friendliness and rapid development capabilities, low-level programming remains essential for several reasons.

1. System Programming

Low-level programming is fundamental in system programming, which includes developing operating systems, device drivers, and embedded systems. Operating systems like Windows, Linux, and macOS rely on low-level code to manage hardware resources and provide essential services to applications.

2. Performance-Critical Applications

Applications that require the highest level of performance, such as real-time systems, game engines, and high-frequency trading platforms, often use low-level programming. By harnessing the exact capabilities of the hardware, developers can optimize their applications for speed and resource management.

3. Embedded Systems

In the growing field of Internet of Things (IoT) and embedded systems, low-level programming is crucial. These systems often operate with limited resources, and low-level languages allow programmers to develop efficient software that can run on small microcontrollers with minimal memory and processing power.

4. Reverse Engineering and Security

Low-level programming is vital in areas such as reverse engineering, malware analysis, and cybersecurity. Understanding how programs interact with hardware at a low level enables security professionals to identify vulnerabilities, analyze threats, and develop robust protection mechanisms.

5. Understanding Computer Architecture

For aspiring developers and engineers, gaining proficiency in low-level programming fosters a deeper understanding of computer architecture and operating systems. This knowledge is invaluable in debugging complex software issues, optimizing performance, and contributing to projects that require a strong understanding of hardware-software interactions.

The Future of Low-Level Programming

As technology evolves, the demand for efficient, performance-oriented solutions persists. While higher-level programming languages continue to rise in popularity due to their ease of use, industries that require precise control over hardware will always require low-level programming skills. Consequently, a hybrid approach, utilizing both high and low-level programming techniques, is increasingly embraced by software engineers.

Furthermore, as artificial intelligence, machine learning, and quantum computing advance, understanding the principles of low-level programming may provide a competitive edge for developers who wish to navigate these complex environments efficiently.

While it may not be the first choice for many developers today, its importance cannot be overstated. Mastery of low-level programming equips programmers with a profound comprehension of computer systems, enabling them to build innovative solutions and tackle challenges in an ever-evolving technological landscape.

Assembly Language and Its Role in Modern Computing

Assembly language, often considered the bridge between machine code and higher-level programming, plays a crucial role in modern computing. This chapter delves into the fundamentals of assembly language, its significance, and its rapidly evolving role in today's technological landscape.

Understanding Assembly Language ### What is Assembly Language?

Assembly language is a low-level programming language that provides a symbolic representation of a computer's machine code. Each assembly language instruction corresponds directly to a machine instruction, making it specific to a particular computer architecture. Assembly languages consist of mnemonics, symbolic names for memory addresses, and operators that represent operations such as arithmetic and logical processes.

Components of Assembly Language

Mnemonics: These are human-readable codes that are used to represent machine-level instructions. For example, `MOV` represents data movement, while `ADD` indicates an addition operation.

Operands: These are the values or addresses the instructions operate on. Operands could be immediate values, memory addresses, or register names.

Directives: Often referred to as pseudo-ops, directives provide information to the assembler but do not translate into machine code. They include commands for defining variables or allocating memory.

Labels: Labels are named references for locations in code that allow for easy jumping and branching in program flow. They help to direct the control flow of the program.

The Assembly Programming Process

The process of programming in assembly language involves several steps:

Writing Code: Programmers craft assembly language code using mnemonics and directives.

Assembling: An assembler converts the assembly code into machine code, preparing it for execution on the hardware.

Linking: The machine code may need to be linked with other code libraries or modules, allowing for a complete program.

Execution: The final machine code is executed by the processor, performing the desired tasks. ## The Significance of Assembly Language

Performance and Efficiency

In an era where computing power and efficiency are paramount, assembly language continues to showcase its advantages. Programs written in assembly can execute significantly faster than those written in high-level languages because they make direct use of hardware capabilities. This efficiency is especially crucial in embedded systems, real-time applications, and high-performance computing where timing and resource management are critical. ### Hardware Control

Assembly language provides developers with granular control over system hardware, including CPU registers and memory management, allowing programmers to optimize their code to utilize system resources effectively. This feature is paramount in operating system development, device drivers, and system utilities.

Learning Fundamental Concepts

For aspiring programmers and computer scientists, learning assembly language introduces fundamental concepts of how computers function at the lowest level. This knowledge can deepen understanding of more abstract programming paradigms, highlight the implications of compiler optimizations, and improve problem-solving skills by fostering a detailed understanding of data handling and memory interactions.

Assembly Language in Modern Computing ### Embedded Systems and IoT

As the Internet of Things (IoT) expands, assembly language remains highly relevant in the development of embedded systems that require efficient resource utilization. Devices such as sensors, microcontrollers, and robotics often utilize assembly code to ensure fast response times and low power consumption.

Performance-Critical Applications

In areas such as gaming, scientific simulations, and financial systems where performance criteria are stringent, assembly language is employed for critical performance sections of code. It allows developers to fine-tune algorithms and optimize routines that would otherwise be inefficient in higher-level languages.

Legacy Code Maintenance

Many systems and applications still operate on legacy codebases written in assembly language. The ability to understand and maintain such code is essential for ongoing support, system upgrades, and integration with newer technologies.

Challenges and Perception

Despite its merits, assembly language is often perceived as difficult and cumbersome compared to modern high-level programming languages. This complexity can deter new developers from learning it. The need for specific knowledge about hardware architecture further complicates the learning curve. Additionally, the longer development time required for assembly programming can be a drawback in fast-paced software environments.

Understanding assembly language provides a powerful lens into the inner workings of computers, offering insights that can enhance programming skills across the spectrum. As technology continues to advance, the importance of assembly language will likely persist, reminding us of the fundamental principles that underpin all computing.

Chapter 2: Setting Up Your Assembly Development Environment

Establishing a strong and efficient assembly development environment is vital for individuals aiming to explore the complex realm of low-level programming. In contrast to high-level programming languages, assembly language necessitates a more direct engagement with the hardware. This chapter will provide guidance on the fundamental aspects of setting up your development environment, ensuring that you possess the appropriate tools and configurations to enhance your productivity.

2.1 Comprehending Assembly Language

Prior to embarking on the setup process, it is important to understand the nature of assembly language. Assembly language acts as a symbolic representation of a computer's machine code, allowing for the creation of programs that interact closely with the hardware. Each CPU architecture is associated with its own specific assembly language, indicating that the selection of tools may differ depending on the architecture you are working with (such as x86, ARM, MIPS, etc.).## 2.2 Choosing the Right Tools ### 2.2.1 Assembler

The first and foremost tool you will need is an assembler. Assemblers convert assembly language code into machine code, enabling the CPU to execute the instructions. Popular assemblers include:

NASM (Netwide Assembler): Known for its simplicity and flexibility, NASM supports a variety of output formats and is widely used for x86 architecture.

MASM (Microsoft Macro Assembler): Ideal for

Windows-based development, MASM is tailored for x86 architecture and offers powerful macros.

GAS (GNU Assembler): Part of the GNU Binutils, GAS is favored for its compatibility with various architectures.

Choose the assembler that best suits your project needs and operating system. You may also want to explore IDEs that have integrated support for specific assemblers.

2.2.2 Debugger

Debugging is an integral part of programming, especially in assembly, where errors can be difficult to trace. A good debugger can simplify the process significantly. Some popular debuggers include:

GDB (GNU Debugger): A powerful debugger compatible with many platforms. It supports remote debugging and can attach to running processes.

OllyDbg: A Windows-based tool focused on analyzing binary programs, OllyDbg is particularly popular among reverse engineers.

Selecting a debugger that matches your assembler and platform can streamline your debugging process. ### 2.2.3 Integrated Development Environment (IDE)

While assembly programming can be done in a simple text editor, an IDE can drastically enhance your workflow with features like syntax highlighting, code completion, and integrated debugging. Notable options include:

Eclipse with CDT: Though primarily a C/C++ IDE, Eclipse can be configured for assembly development with plugins.

Visual Studio: Widely used in the Windows

environment, Visual Studio has excellent support for MASM.

VS Code: A lightweight editor that can be customized for various languages, including assembly, with the right extensions.

Pick an IDE that aligns with your comfort level and the demands of your project. ## 2.3 Setting Up Your Environment

2.3.1 Installing Your Tools

To get started, download and install the necessary tools based on your choices above.

Assembler: Follow the instructions on the homepage of your chosen assembler. Make sure to add its binary directory to your system's PATH for easier access via the command line.

Debugger: Download the installer or binary distribution of the debugger. Ensure that it is compatible with your operating system.

IDE: If you chose an IDE, download and install it, making sure to configure it to utilize the assembler and debugger.

2.3.2 Environment Variables

Configuring environment variables may be necessary to ensure that the command line can locate your assembler and debugger. For example, on Windows, you can set environment variables by navigating to System Properties > Advanced > Environment Variables. On Unix-based systems, you can edit your

`.bashrc` or `.bash_profile` to include:

```bash
export PATH=$PATH:/path/to/your/assembler export PATH=$PATH:/path/to/your/debugger
```

2.3.3 Creating Your Workspace

Choose a directory structure for your projects. A clean and organized setup can substantially enhance your coding efficiency. Consider creating a base workspace with subdirectories for each project, including:

src: For all source code files.

bin: For compiled binaries.

obj: For object files produced during compilation.

debug: For files related to debugging. ## 2.4 Testing Your Setup

Once everything is installed and configured, it's time to verify that your environment is functioning correctly. Write a simple "Hello, World!" program in assembly to test the setup. Here's an example for NASM:

```assembly
section .data

msg db 'Hello, World!',0

section .text global _start

_start:

; write our string to stdout

mov eax, 4    ; syscall number for sys_write mov ebx, 1; file descriptor 1 is stdout mov ecx, msg        ; pointer
```

to the string

```
mov edx, 13          ; length of the string int 0x80      ;
call kernel

; exit

mov eax, 1     ; syscall number for sys_exit xor ebx, ebx ;
exit code 0

int 0x80       ; call kernel
```

Compile and run it. In NASM, you would use:

```bash
nasm -f elf32 hello.asm -o hello.o ld -m elf_i386 -s -o hello
hello.o

./hello
```

If you see "Hello, World!" printed to the screen, congratulations! Your assembly development environment is ready.

With your assembly development environment now properly configured, you're ready to explore the depths of assembly programming. The tools and techniques you've set up will play a pivotal role in your journey, allowing you to write, debug, and execute assembly programs effectively.

Choosing an Assembler: NASM, MASM, GAS, and Others

The choice of an assembler can significantly influence not only the development process but also the performance and portability of the resulting programs. This chapter will explore some of the most popular assemblers in use today—NASM, MASM, GAS, and others—highlighting their features, advantages, and specific use cases to help you make an informed decision.

Understanding Assemblers

Before diving into the specifics of each assembler, it is essential to understand what an assembler does. At its core, an assembler translates assembly language, which consists of mnemonic instructions, into machine code—binary instructions that the CPU can execute. Assemblers may also perform optimization and macro processing, helping to streamline and enhance the code's efficiency.

Assemblers can be categorized into two main types:

Single-pass Assemblers: These translate the source code in one pass, making them faster but potentially limited in their ability to resolve symbolic references.

Multi-pass Assemblers: These make multiple passes over the source code, enabling them to resolve forward references and perform more complex optimizations.

NASM (Netwide Assembler) ### Overview

NASM is an open-source assembler that has gained popularity due to its simplicity, versatility, and adherence to the x86 architecture. It's suitable for both beginners and professionals and is known for its straightforward syntax.

Features

Cross-platform: NASM runs on various operating systems, including Windows, Linux, and macOS.

Modular Design: It supports various output formats like ELF, COFF, and Mach-O, making it easy to integrate with different environments.

Rich Documentation: NASM has comprehensive documentation, making it accessible for learners and experienced programmers alike.

Support for 16-bit, 32-bit, and 64-bit architectures: This versatility allows developers to port applications easily across different systems.

Use Cases

NASM is particularly well-suited for systems programming, kernel development, and application programming where performance is critical. It's commonly used in the development of operating systems and embedded systems.

MASM (Microsoft Macro Assembler) ### Overview

MASM is a powerful assembler developed by Microsoft, primarily designed for the Windows platform. It offers advanced features that streamline assembly programming and is ideal for developers working on projects within the Microsoft ecosystem.

Features

Integrated Macro Facilities: MASM includes advanced macro capabilities, allowing for more complex and readable code.

Toolchain Integration: As part of the Microsoft development environment, MASM integrates seamlessly with tools like Visual Studio, enhancing productivity.

High-Level Language Support: MASM supports high-level constructs (like procedures and structures) that make assembly programming easier for developers accustomed to languages like C/C++.

Use Cases

MASM is often employed in Windows application development, game programming, and performance-sensitive applications where direct hardware interaction is required.

GAS (GNU Assembler) ### Overview

GAS is the assembler for the GNU (GNU's Not Unix!) project and is part of the GNU Binutils package. It supports various architectures and is widely used in conjunction with the GCC (GNU Compiler Collection).

Features

Cross-Platform Support: GAS is highly portable and can be run on numerous platforms, making it suitable for cross-compilation.

Integrated with GCC: When used with GCC, GAS can leverage the optimizations provided by the compiler, resulting in efficient code generation.

Support for AT&T and Intel Syntax: GAS allows developers to choose between two syntaxes, catering to personal or project preferences.

Use Cases

GAS is particularly popular in Linux development and is often used for building system-level software, drivers, and applications requiring compliance with POSIX standards.

Other Assemblers

While NASM, MASM, and GAS dominate the landscape, several other assemblers are worth mentioning:

FASM (Flat Assembler): Known for its speed and minimalistic design, FASM is an open-source assembler that emphasizes simplicity, direct encoding, and macro capabilities.

TASM (Turbo Assembler): Developed by Borland, TASM supports extensive macro features and compatibility with Turbo C, making it a popular choice among embedded systems developers.

HLA (High-Level Assembly): This assembler allows developers to write in a higher-level syntax while still compiling down to assembly, making it suitable for educational purposes.

Choosing the right assembler is a critical decision that can impact the trajectory of your development projects. NASM, MASM, and GAS each have their strengths, catering to different programming environments and personal preferences. Consider factors such as target architecture, project requirements, development environment, and your own level of expertise when selecting an assembler.

Installing and Configuring Your First Assembly Programming Setup

Unlike high-level programming languages, which hide the complexities of the machine, assembly language allows programmers to write instructions that are closely related to the architecture of the underlying hardware. This makes assembly particularly useful for performance-critical applications, system programming, and understanding how computers work at a fundamental level.

Before you dive into the code, it's important to set up your development environment. This chapter will guide you through installing the necessary software and configuring your system for assembly programming.

1.1 Choosing the Right Assembly Language

Assembly languages are specifically designed for different computer architectures. Popular choices include:

x86 Assembly: Widely used for Intel and AMD processors.

ARM Assembly: Common in mobile devices and embedded systems.

MIPS Assembly: Often used in academic settings to teach the principles of computer architecture.

Identify the architecture for which you wish to develop, as this will influence your choice of assembler and toolchain.

1.2 Installing an Assembler

An assembler is a program that translates assembly

language code into machine code. Here we will outline the installation for two popular assemblers: NASM (Netwide Assembler) and GNU Assembler (GAS).

1.2.1 Installing NASM

Download NASM:

Visit the [NASM official website](https://www.nasm.us) to download the latest version suitable for your operating system.

Install NASM:

For Windows, run the installer and follow the prompts.

For macOS, you can install NASM using Homebrew with the command:

```bash
brew install nasm
```

For Linux, install NASM using your distribution's package manager. For example, on Ubuntu, you can use:

```bash
sudo apt install nasm
```

Verify Installation:

Open your terminal or command prompt and type:

```bash nasm -v
```

You should see the version of NASM printed if the installation was successful. ### 1.2.2 Installing GNU Assembler (GAS)

GAS is part of the GNU Binutils package, which is usually pre-installed on Linux distributions. For development on Windows, you can install it as part of the MinGW or Cygwin packages.

Windows:

Download and install [MinGW](http://www.mingw.org) or [Cygwin](https://www.cygwin.com/).

During installation, make sure to include the development tools that provide access to the GNU assembler.

Linux:

Usually pre-installed. If not, use:

```bash
sudo apt install binutils
```

macOS:

GNU tools can be installed using Homebrew:

```bash
brew install binutils
```

Verify Installation:

Type the following command in the terminal:

```bash
```

as --version
```

Check that the version information appears correctly. ## 1.3 Setting Up a Code Editor

While you can use any text editor to write assembly code, a code editor with syntax highlighting and debugging features can significantly enhance your coding experience. Popular options include:

- **Visual Studio Code**: A powerful and popular editor that supports extensions for assembly language.

**Install Visual Studio Code**:

Download it from the [official website](https://code.visualstudio.com).

Install and open the application.

**Set Up Assembly Language Support**:

Open the extensions panel (Ctrl+Shift+X).

Search for "x86 and x86_64 Assembly" and install the extension that supports assembly language syntax highlighting.

## 1.4 Creating Your First Assembly Program

Now that your environment is set up, let's create our first assembly program.

**Create a New File**:

Open your code editor and create a new file named `hello.asm`.
```

Write the Code:

Add the following simple code to display "Hello, World!" (for NASM):

```assembly
section .data
hello db 'Hello, World!',0

section .text global _start

_start:
; write our string to stdout
mov rax, 1          ; syscall number for sys_write mov rdi, 1   ; file descriptor 1 is stdout mov rsi, hello
        ; pointer to string
mov rdx, 13   ; length of string
syscall; invoke operating system to do the write
; exit the program
mov rax, 60          ; syscall number for sys_exit xor rdi, rdi      ; exit code 0
syscall
```

Assemble and Link the Program:

Open the terminal and navigate to the directory where your `hello.asm` file is located. Run the following commands:

```bash
nasm -f elf64 hello.asm ld -s -o hello hello.o
```

34

Run Your Program:

Execute the program by typing:

```bash
./hello
```

You should see the output:

```
Hello, World!
```

1.5 Troubleshooting Common Setup Issues

Assembler Not Found: Ensure that the assembler installation path is included in your system's `PATH` environment variable.

Syntax Errors: Ensure that your assembly code follows the conventions of the assembler you are using. Syntax can vary between NASM and GAS.

Permission Denied: If you get a permission error while running your program, check the execute permissions of the compiled binary using `chmod +x hello`.

This chapter has laid the foundation for your assembly development environment, and the following chapters will expand on writing more complex programs, debugging, and optimizing your code. Get ready to dive into the intricacies of the machine and unleash the power of assembly language!

Chapter 3: Understanding the CPU and Registers

The central processing unit (CPU) is the brain of a computer system. It performs the essential tasks of processing data, executing instructions, and managing the flow of information within the machine. Assembly programming operates at the hardware level, allowing programmers to write instructions that communicate directly with the CPU. In this chapter, we will explore the architecture and function of the CPU, as well as the critical role of registers in assembly programming.

3.1 The Architecture of the CPU ### 3.1.1 Components of the CPU

The CPU comprises several key components that work together to execute instructions:

Control Unit (CU): The control unit directs the operation of the CPU. It retrieves and decodes instructions from memory, orchestrates their execution, and manages the flow of data to and from other hardware components.

Arithmetic Logic Unit (ALU): The ALU performs arithmetic and logical operations. It handles tasks such as addition, subtraction, multiplication, division, and logical comparisons (like AND, OR, NOT).

Registers: Registers are high-speed storage locations within the CPU that temporarily hold data, instructions, or addresses. They are crucial for speeding up data access for the ALU and providing immediate data for processing.

Cache Memory: The CPU cache is a small amount of

high-speed memory located close to the CPU, used to store frequently accessed data and instructions to reduce latency.

3.1.2 Instruction Cycle

The CPU follows a specific cycle when executing instructions, commonly known as the *fetch-decode-execute* cycle:

Fetch: The control unit fetches the next instruction from memory, using the program counter (PC) to track the current instruction's location.

Decode: The fetched instruction is decoded to determine the operation to be performed, the operands involved, and any addressing modes.

Execute: The CPU executes the instruction, which may involve performing calculations, modifying data in registers, or interacting with other components like memory.

Store: Finally, the result of the execution is stored back in memory or written to a register. ## 3.2 Understanding Registers

Registers are the fastest memory accessible to the CPU and are crucial in optimizing performance. They serve various purposes, including holding data for immediate processing, storing results, and managing addresses for memory access.

3.2.1 Types of Registers

General Purpose Registers (GPRs): These registers can store both data and addresses. They can be accessed and manipulated freely by assembly instructions, making them versatile for different operations.

Special Purpose Registers: These include:

Program Counter (PC): Holds the memory address of the next instruction to be executed.

Stack Pointer (SP): Points to the current top of the stack, used for managing function calls and local variables.

Instruction Register (IR): Holds the currently executing instruction.

Status Register / Flags: Contains flags that signal the outcome of operations, such as zero (if the result is zero), carry (if there was a carry from an arithmetic operation), and overflow (if an arithmetic overflow occurs).

Floating-Point Registers: Used for operations involving floating-point numbers, these registers optimize calculations with real numbers beyond the integer arithmetic that general-purpose registers handle.

3.2.2 Register Operations

In assembly language, registers are accessed using specific instructions. Common operations include:

Load: Loading data from memory to a register (e.g., `MOV` instruction).

Store: Moving data from a register back to memory (e.g., `MOV` instruction).

Arithmetic Operations: Performing calculations directly within registers (e.g., `ADD`, `SUB`).

Logical Operations: Performing logical operations (e.g., `AND`, `OR`, `XOR`).

Choosing the right register for specific operations is a key aspect of efficient programming. The limited number of registers means that clever usage can lead to significant performance improvements.

3.3 Programming with Registers

To illustrate the importance of registers in assembly programming, let's discuss a simple example. Consider a task to add two numbers and store the result.

Example: Basic Addition

```assembly
; Example of adding two numbers in Assembly section
.data

num1 db 5    ; First number num2 db 10        ;    Second number

result db 0    ; Placeholder for result

section .text global _start

_start:

; Load num1 into register AL

mov al, [num1] ; Move the value of num1 into AL

; Load num2 into register BL

mov bl, [num2] ; Move the value of num2 into BL

; Add values in AL and BL, store in AL add al, bl; AL = AL + BL

; Store the result in memory
```

mov [result], al ; Move the sum from AL to result

; Exit program

mov eax, 60 ; syscall: exit xor edi, edi ; return 0 syscall
```

In this example, we use two general-purpose registers (AL and BL) for addition. The use of registers allows for direct manipulation of data, making the operation efficient.

Understanding the CPU and its registers is fundamental to mastering assembly programming. By leveraging the architecture and the various types of registers, programmers can write more efficient and effective code.

# CPU Architecture and How Assembly Interacts with Hardware

This chapter aims to unravel the intricacies of CPU architecture and examine how assembly language serves as a bridge between high-level programming languages and the underlying hardware.

## 1. Overview of CPU Architecture

The CPU is primarily composed of several key components, each with distinct functions that facilitate processing tasks. The basic architecture of a CPU can be divided into the following components:

### 1.1. ALU (Arithmetic Logic Unit)

The ALU is responsible for performing all arithmetic and logical operations. It executes operations such as addition, subtraction, bitwise AND/OR operations, and
```

comparisons. It does so based on the instructions provided, which are typically encoded in binary.

1.2. Control Unit (CU)

The Control Unit orchestrates the overall operation of the CPU. It interprets the instructions from the memory and signals the appropriate components within the CPU to perform actions. The CU is fundamental in managing the instruction cycle, which includes fetching, decoding, executing, and storing results.

1.3. Registers

Registers are small, high-speed storage locations within the CPU that temporarily hold data and instructions. They significantly enhance processing speed by reducing the need to access slower main memory. Common registers include the accumulator, index registers, and program counter (PC), which tracks the address of the next instruction to be executed.

1.4. Cache Memory

Cache memory serves as a buffer between the CPU and main memory. It stores frequently accessed data and instructions, thereby accelerating the execution time by reducing latency. CPU caches are typically organized in levels (L1, L2, L3), where L1 is the smallest and fastest.

1.5. Buses

Buses are communication pathways that connect different components of the CPU and the rest of the computer system, including RAM and input/output devices. The primary types of buses are data buses (transport data), address buses (transport addresses), and control buses (transport control signals).

2. Instruction Set Architecture (ISA)

The Instruction Set Architecture (ISA) is a fundamental aspect of CPU design. It defines the set of instructions that the CPU can understand and execute, along with the corresponding data types, addressing modes, and registers. ISAs can be classified into two main categories:

2.1. CISC (Complex Instruction Set Computer)

CISC architectures, such as x86, provide a large number of instructions, allowing complex operations to be performed in a single instruction cycle. This can lead to more efficient coding but can also result in longer execution times due to the complexity of decoding these instructions.

2.2. RISC (Reduced Instruction Set Computer)

RISC architectures, such as ARM, prioritize a smaller set of simpler instructions that can be executed in a single clock cycle. This simplicity lends itself to higher performance and easier pipelining, which allows multiple instruction stages to be processed simultaneously.

3. Assembly Language: The Intersection Between Software and Hardware

Assembly language acts as a thin layer between high-level programming and machine code, enabling programmers to write instructions in a more understandable form. Each assembly instruction typically corresponds to a single machine instruction, allowing for direct control over hardware.

3.1. Syntax of Assembly Language

Assembly language syntax varies depending on the

architecture, but most include:

Mnemonics: Human-readable representations of machine instructions (e.g., `MOV`, `ADD`, `SUB`).

Operands: Variables, constants, or register names on which operations are performed.

Labels: Named references to memory addresses, enabling more organized code.

For example, an assembly instruction like `MOV AX, 5` transfers the value `5` into the register `AX`. ### 3.2. Interaction with Hardware

When an assembly program is executed, the following sequence of operations typically occurs:

Assembly: The assembly code is translated into machine code by an assembler, generating binary instructions that the CPU can execute.

Loading into Memory: The machine code is loaded into main memory, where the CPU can access it.

Execution: The CPU fetches the instructions from memory, decodes them via the Control Unit, and executes them using the ALU or other components. The results of these operations may also be stored back in memory or sent to output devices.

This process demonstrates how assembly language provides granular control over the CPU's hardware, allowing programmers to optimize performance and resource utilization.

4. Low-Level Programming and Optimization

Understanding the intricacies of CPU architecture and

assembly language allows developers to write highly efficient code, optimizing for speed and memory usage. Here are several key strategies:

4.1. Leveraging Registers

Utilizing registers effectively can significantly boost performance. For example, keeping frequently used variables in registers rather than memory can reduce access times considerably.

4.2. Minimizing Instruction Cycles

By simplifying algorithmic logic and restructuring assembly instructions, programmers can reduce the number of cycles needed for execution. Techniques such as loop unrolling or instruction reordering can enhance performance in performance-critical applications.

4.3. Understanding Memory Hierarchy

Efficient memory usage is vital for performance. Knowledge of cache architecture and memory locality principles can help developers design algorithms that take advantage of faster-access memory locations.

By understanding the roles of the ALU, Control Unit, registers, and memory hierarchy, alongside the principles of assembly language, programmers are better equipped to harness the full power of computer hardware. This synergy between low-level programming and hardware interaction paves the way for writing efficient, high-performance applications that can leverage the capabilities of modern CPUs.

Working with Registers: General-Purpose, Special-Purpose, and Segment Registers

In assembly programming, understanding how to work with these registers is crucial for optimizing performance, writing efficient code, and interacting directly with the hardware. This chapter will delve into the different types of registers—general-purpose, special-purpose, and segment registers—highlighting their functions, uses, and significance in assembly language programming.

1. Understanding Registers

Registers are small storage locations that reside within the CPU. Unlike RAM, which provides slower access speeds and larger storage, registers are specifically designed for temporary data storage and manipulation needed during instruction execution. The number of registers and their capabilities can vary significantly between different CPU architectures.

1.1 The Role of Registers

The primary roles of registers include:

Data Storage: Registers temporarily hold data that the CPU is currently processing.

Instruction Execution: Many CPU instructions directly operate on register values, making it essential for programmers to effectively utilize them.

Addressing Modes: Registers can hold addresses to memory locations, allowing the CPU to fetch or modify data at specific memory addresses.

2. General-Purpose Registers (GPRs) ### 2.1 Definition and Purpose

General-purpose registers (GPRs) are versatile and can store any form of data, be it integers, floating-point numbers, or addresses. They are used in a variety of operations, including arithmetic calculations, data movement, and control operations.

2.2 Common General-Purpose Registers

In the x86 architecture, some common general-purpose registers include:

EAX (Accumulator): Primarily used for arithmetic operations and function return values.

EBX (Base Register): Often used as a pointer to data in memory.

ECX (Counter Register): Used for loop counters and string operations.

EDX (Data Register): Utilized for I/O operations and as an extended storage during multiplication and division.

2.3 Usage of GPRs

The versatility of GPRs allows programmers to choose registers based on their needs. For example, when performing a series of calculations, a programmer might use EAX to hold intermediate results and utilize ECX to control the number of iterations in a loop.

Example

```assembly
mov eax, 5    ; Load 5 into EAX mov ebx, 10            ; Load 10 into EBX

add eax, ebx  ; EAX = EAX + EBX (EAX now contains 15)
```

```
```

3. Special-Purpose Registers ### 3.1 Definition

Special-purpose registers (SPRs) are designed for specific functions and typically include status and control information about the CPU. They play a critical role in the execution and control flow of programs.

3.2 Key Special-Purpose Registers

Instruction Pointer (IP or EIP): Points to the next instruction to be executed.

Stack Pointer (SP or ESP): Points to the top of the stack in memory, managing function calls and local variables.

Base Pointer (BP or EBP): Points to the base of the current stack frame, facilitating the access of function parameters and local variables.

Flag Register (FLAGS): Holds flags that indicate the status of the CPU (e.g., zero flag, carry flag) and control the execution flow.

3.3 Usage of SPRs

Special-purpose registers are instrumental in managing program execution flow. The instruction pointer is updated automatically after each instruction execution, while the stack pointer and base pointer help manage function calls and local variables efficiently.

Example

```assembly
push eax      ; Push EAX onto the stack
```

```
call my_function    ; Call a function which modifies the
stack pop eax; Restore EAX after the function returns
```

4. Segment Registers ### 4.1 Definition

Segment registers are used primarily in segmented memory architectures, such as the x86 architecture. They define the starting address of different segments, such as code, data, and stack segments. This segmentation helps manage memory more efficiently, especially in systems with limited address space.

4.2 Key Segment Registers

CS (Code Segment): Points to the segment containing the executable code.

DS (Data Segment): Points to the segment containing data variables.

SS (Stack Segment): Points to the segment used for the stack, crucial for dynamic memory allocation during program execution.

ES, FS, GS: Additional segment registers that can be utilized for specific data segments. ### 4.3 Usage of Segment Registers Segment registers facilitate organized memory access, enabling distinctions between different types of data and instructions. Proper management and understanding of segment registers can lead to more efficient memory utilization.

Example

```assembly
mov ax, ds    ; Load the data segment address into AX
```

```
mov bx, [ax] ; Access a data variable using the data
segment
```
```
```
Understanding and effectively utilizing general-purpose, special-purpose, and segment registers is a key skill in assembly programming. These registers are the building blocks of CPU operations, affecting everything from arithmetic calculations to memory management. Mastery over register usage enables programmers to write efficient, high-performance code and to interact closely with the underlying hardware.

Chapter 4: Assembly Language Syntax and Structure

This chapter delves into the key components of assembly language syntax, the structure of assembly programs, and common conventions that programmers follow to write effective and maintainable assembly code.

4.1 Basic Components of Assembly Language

At the heart of assembly language are several fundamental components that every assembly programmer must understand:

4.1.1 Instructions

Instructions are the fundamental operations that the processor can perform, such as data movement, arithmetic calculations, logical operations, and control flow. Each instruction corresponds to a specific machine code operation and typically consists of an operation code (opcode) followed by operands. For example:

```
```

```
MOV AX, 1
```

```
```

In this instruction, `MOV` is the opcode indicating a move operation, `AX` is a specific register, and `1` is the value being moved into that register.

4.1.2 Operands

Operands are the entities that the instruction manipulates. They can be immediate values (like constants), register names, or memory addresses. Understanding the types of operands you can use is crucial for writing effective assembly programs. For instance, in the instruction `ADD BX, [1234h]`, `BX` is a register and `[1234h]` is a memory address containing the value to be added.

4.1.3 Labels

Labels are placeholders used to identify positions in the code or data and provide a way to reference them in instructions. Labels enable easier navigation within the program and are critical for control flow, such as jumps and loops. A label is defined by placing a name followed by a colon:

``` start:

MOV AX, 5
```

4.1.4 Directives

Directives inform the assembler about how to process the program, often indicating the beginning and end of code, defining data, or setting up memory space. Common directives include `.data`, `.code`, and `.org`.

Directives do not correspond to machine instructions but tell the assembler how to organize the code and data segments:

```
.data

counter DB 10
```

4.1.5 Comments

Comments allow programmers to include explanatory text that is not executed as part of the code. They are critical for maintaining code readability. In most assembly languages, comments can be indicated with a semicolon (`;`):

```
```

```
; This adds two numbers
ADD AX, BX  ; AX = AX + BX
```

```
```

4.2 Structure of an Assembly Language Program

An assembly program typically follows a specific structure, which enhances readability and maintainability. The general structure is often segmented into three main sections: data segment, code segment, and sometimes stack segment.

4.2.1 Data Segment

The data segment is where all variables and constants used in the program are defined. This section allocates memory for data and can include various data types, including BYTE, WORD, and DWORD, depending on the architecture.

```
```

```
.data
message DB 'Hello, World!',0
```

```
```

4.2.2 Code Segment

The code segment houses the executable instructions of

the program. It begins with a directive indicating the start of the code and contains the actual logic of the assembly program.

```
```

.code main:

MOV DX, offset message MOV AH, 09h

INT 21h RET

```
```

4.2.3 Stack Segment

Some assembly languages provide a stack segment, which manages memory for temporary data during execution. It's crucial for function calls, local variables, and system stack management.

```
```

.stack 100h

```
```

4.3 Common Assembly Language Conventions

While assembly language offers flexibility, adherence to certain conventions improves code clarity and maintainability.

4.3.1 Naming Conventions

Consistent naming conventions for labels and variables can significantly enhance readability. Common practices include using descriptive names and prefacing them with an indication of their type (e.g., "var_" for variables).

4.3.2 Indentation and Formatting

Proper indentation and spacing help separate logical blocks of code and make instructions easier to read. It's a good practice to align similar instructions and maintain uniform spacing.

4.3.3 Modular Design

Breaking code into modular segments, such as procedures or functions, promotes reusability and simplifies debugging. Each procedure should perform a single, well-defined task and can be called from various points within the program.

4.3.4 Documentation

Thorough documentation of the code through comments and external documentation files helps future developers (or yourself) understand the logic and flow of the program. This is particularly important in assembly language due to its low-level nature.

By mastering the basic components of instructions, operands, labels, and directives, programmers can create structured and efficient assembly programs. Adhering to best practices in naming, formatting, and documentation will lead to more maintainable and understandable assembly code, which is especially useful in complex projects.

Writing Your First Assembly Program: Structure and Components

In this chapter, we will explore the essential structure and components of an assembly program, guiding you through the process of writing your first assembly program from scratch.

Understanding Assembly Language

Before diving into the practical aspects of writing an assembly program, let's take a moment to understand some fundamental concepts:

Architecture: Assembly language is specific to a computer architecture. Common architectures include x86, ARM, and MIPS. The instructions and syntax vary between different architectures.

Assembler: An assembler is a tool that translates assembly language code into machine code. Each assembly instruction corresponds to a specific machine code instruction executable by the CPU.

Registers: Registers are small storage locations within the CPU that hold data temporarily. They are crucial for performing operations efficiently.

Instruction Set: The collection of instructions that a CPU can execute is referred to as the instruction set. Assembly languages are designed around these instruction sets, providing mnemonic representations of machine code.

Components of an Assembly Program

An assembly program consists of several components that work together to create a meaningful application. Here are the key components you should be aware of when writing your program:

1. **Comments**

Comments are annotations in your code that are ignored by the assembler. They are essential for documenting your code and explaining its logic. In most assembly languages, comments begin with a semicolon (`;`). For example:

```assembly
; This program adds two numbers and stores the result
```

2. **Labels**

Labels are identifiers that mark specific locations in your code, allowing you to reference them easily. They usually appear at the beginning of a line and are followed by a colon. For instance:

```assembly
start:
mov ax, 1
```

3. **Instructions**

Instructions form the core of your assembly program. They dictate the operations to be performed, such as data movement, arithmetic, and control flow. Each instruction generally consists of an operation code (opcode) and operands. For example:

```assembly
mov ax, bx ; Move the value from register bx to register ax
add ax, 5  ; Add 5 to the value in register ax
```

4. **Data Section**

The data section is where you define variables and allocate memory for your program's data. You will typically declare your data at the beginning of the program. For example:

```assembly
section .data
```

```
number1 db 5      ; Define  byte  variable  number1
number2 db 10          ; Define byte variable number2
```

5. **Code Section**

The code section contains the executable instructions of your program. This is where you implement the logic of your application. You will define this section using a specific directive, such as `section .text`:

```assembly
section .text
```

global _start ; Specify the entry point for the program

_start:

; Your code goes here

```
```

6. **Directives**

Directives are commands that guide the assembler on how to process the code. They do not result in machine code but affect the way the assembler behaves. Common directives include `global` for defining global symbols and `section` for separating different parts of the code or data.

Writing Your First Assembly Program

Now that we've discussed the basic components of an assembly program, let's put it all together and write a simple program that adds two numbers and prints the result:

Step 1: Setting Up the Environment

Install an Assembler: Depending on the architecture you are using (x86, x64, ARM), choose an assembler like NASM (Netwide Assembler) for x86 architecture.

Create a New File: Open your text editor and create a new file named `add.asm`. ### Step 2: Writing the Code

Here's a complete example of an assembly program that adds two numbers:

```assembly
section .data

number1 db 5        ; First number number2 db 10
        ; Second number

result db 0    ; Variable to store the result

section .text

global _start ; Required for linking

_start:

mov al, [number1]        ; Load the value of number1 into register al add al, [number2] ; Add the value of number2 to al

mov [result], al     ; Store the result in the result variable

; Exit the program

mov eax, 60          ; sys_exit syscall number xor edi, edi
        ; Exit code 0

syscall
```

```
```

Step 3: Assembling and Running the Program

Assemble the Program: Open your terminal and run the following command:

```bash
nasm -f elf64 -o add.o add.asm
```

Link the Program: Link the object file to create an executable:

```bash
ld -o add add.o
```

Run the Program: Finally, execute the program:

```bash
./add
```

You have successfully written, assembled, and executed your first assembly program. Writing in assembly can be challenging at first, but with practice, you will gain a deeper understanding of how computers operate at the hardware level.

Directives, Labels, and Comments: Organizing Your Code

While it allows for precise control of hardware, writing assembly code can quickly become complex and challenging to maintain. To enhance readability and organization, effective use of directives, labels, and comments is essential. In this chapter, we will discuss the pivotal roles that these components play in assembly programming and how they contribute to writing clean, understandable, and maintainable code.

1. Understanding Directives

Directives are non-executable instructions that give the assembler hints on how to process the following code. They are crucial for defining data, allocating memory, and controlling certain aspects of the assembly process. While the exact syntax and functionality of directives can vary between different assembly languages and assemblers, their purpose remains largely similar.

1.1 Defining Data

One of the primary uses of directives is to define and allocate memory for data. For example, in x86 assembly using the NASM (Netwide Assembler), you might see directives like:

```assembly
section .data

message db 'Hello, World!', 0
```

Here, `.data` is a directive indicating a section where initialized data is stored. `db` tells the assembler to allocate a byte for each character along with a null terminator. This makes it clear to anyone reading the code which data is being defined and how it will be used later.

60

1.2 Control Flow Directives

Directives such as `.section`, `.text`, and `.bss` are used to indicate different segments of the program's memory. The `.text` section typically contains executable code, while `.bss` usually contains uninitialized data. For instance:

```assembly
section .text global _start

_start:

; code goes here
```

Here, `global _start` marks the entry point of the program, explicitly stated by the programmer. Using sections effectively helps in organizing code into logical sections, making it easier to navigate.

2. Utilizing Labels

Labels are markers used to identify a particular point in your assembly code. They serve as references to code locations, facilitating branching and looping constructs. A label can be defined simply by writing an identifier followed by a colon. For example:

```assembly
start_loop:

; loop code here jmp start_loop
```

In this example, `start_loop:` is a label indicating the start of a loop. The `jmp` instruction uses this label to create an infinite loop. Labels can simplify complex control flow by allowing programmers to refer to various parts of their code without using raw memory addresses.

2.1 Label Naming Conventions

To maintain clarity and avoid confusion, it's important to adhere to consistent naming conventions for labels. Use descriptive names that reflect their purpose; for instance, `function_start:` or `loop_counter:` instead of generic names like `label1:`. This practice helps anyone reading the code to quickly understand its structure and flow.

3. The Power of Comments

Comments are essential for any programming language but hold particular importance in assembly, where the code can be difficult to understand at first glance. Comments allow you to describe what specific blocks of code do, why certain decisions were made, and any underlying logic that might not be immediately apparent.

3.1 Writing Effective Comments

In assembly language, comments typically begin with a semicolon (`;`). Here's a simple example:

```
```assembly section .text global _start

_start:

; Print the message to the console mov eax, 4    ;    syscall: sys_write

mov ebx, 1    ; file descriptor 1: stdout mov ecx, message; pointer to message mov edx, 13         ; message length

int 0x80    ; call kernel
```
```

In this snippet, comments clearly describe the intention behind each instruction. This explanatory layer not only aids others in understanding your code but also allows you, the original author, to recall your logic more easily when reviewing after time has passed.

3.2 Avoiding Comment Overload

While comments are beneficial, over-commenting can lead to clutter and confusion. Aim for a balance: provide enough context to clarify complex logic or non-obvious decisions without stating the obvious. Aim for clarity and brevity.

4. Best Practices for Organizing Your Code

When writing assembly code, consider the following best practices for organization:

Use Sections Wisely: Structure your program with clear sections for data, code, and uninitialized data. It makes your assembly code easier to follow.

Consistent Indentation: Ensure that your code is consistently indented across and within sections. Indentation helps visually separate different logical blocks of code.

Meaningful Names: Use meaningful names for labels and variables, aiming to summarize their purpose or functionality succinctly.

Strategic Comments: Comment your code thoughtfully; keep comments relevant and useful. Focus on explaining why rather than what, especially for complex logic.

Modular Coding: Break down large routines into smaller, more manageable functions or procedures, each with its corresponding labels and comments.

In assembly programming, clear organization through the use of directives, labels, and comments is not merely helpful—it is essential. By mastering these elements, you can enhance the readability and maintainability of your code, making it more accessible not just for others, but also for yourself in the future.

Chapter 5: Memory Management in Assembly

This chapter delves into the fundamentals of memory management in assembly language, covering concepts such as memory organization, segmentation, addressing modes, and efficient memory usage.

5.1 Understanding Memory Organization

To effectively manage memory in assembly language, it is essential to comprehend the structure of computer memory. Memory can be divided into several segments, which typically include:

Code Segment: This area contains the executable instructions of the program.

Data Segment: This segment holds static variables and data used by the program.

Heap Segment: This is a dynamic memory area used for dynamic memory allocation during program execution.

Stack Segment: The stack segment is utilized for function calls and local variable storage, allowing for efficient data management during program execution.

Assembly language provides mechanisms to define and manipulate these segments directly, giving programmers precise control over how their programs utilize memory.

5.2 Addressing Modes

Assembly language supports various addressing modes that allow for different methods of accessing data in memory. Understanding these modes is crucial for effective memory management:

Immediate Addressing: The operand is specified explicitly in the instruction, allowing for direct data manipulation. For example, `MOV AL, 5` moves the value `5` directly into the register `AL`.

Direct Addressing: The instruction specifies a direct memory address where the data is located. For instance, `MOV AL, [1234h]` retrieves data from memory location `0x1234`.

Indirect Addressing: The address of the operand is held in a register or memory location. For example,

`MOV AL, [BX]` retrieves data from the address pointed to by the register `BX`.

Indexed Addressing: This mode uses a base address plus an offset to access memory. It enables accessing arrays efficiently. For instance, `MOV AL, [SI + 10]` accesses the memory location pointed to by

`SI` plus an offset of `10`.

Familiarity with these addressing modes allows assembly programmers to manipulate memory effectively and adapt to various programming scenarios.

5.3 Stack Management

The stack is a crucial data structure in memory management, particularly for storing local variables and maintaining function call information. In assembly, push and pop operations manage the stack effectively:

PUSH Operation: This operation adds a value to the top of the stack, decreasing the stack pointer. For example, `PUSH AX` places the value of `AX` onto the stack.

POP Operation: This retrieves the top value from the stack, increasing the stack pointer. For example,

`POP BX` removes the top value and stores it in `BX`.

The stack operates on a Last In, First Out (LIFO) principle, making it ideal for managing function calls, local variables, and temporary data.

5.4 Dynamic Memory Allocation

Dynamic memory allocation in assembly is significantly different from high-level languages. While high-level languages provide built-in functions to manage memory, assembly requires explicit handling.

Programmers often use the heap for dynamic memory management, employing system calls or library functions to request and release memory.

For instance, in a Windows environment, using `HeapAlloc` and `HeapFree` can help allocate and deallocate memory dynamically. It is crucial to keep track of allocated memory to avoid leaks, ensuring that every allocation has a corresponding deallocation.

5.5 Efficient Memory Usage

Efficient memory management is critical for optimizing program performance and preventing resource exhaustion. Here are several strategies for effective memory usage in assembly language:

Minimize Fragmentation: When allocating memory, prefer larger contiguous blocks rather than many smaller allocations. Fragmentation can lead to inefficient use of memory.

Free Unused Memory: Always ensure that

dynamically allocated memory is freed when no longer needed. This helps prevent memory leaks, which can degrade performance and crash the program.

Use Local Variables: Whenever possible, utilize the stack for local variables, as this allows for automatic management and quicker access compared to heap-allocated variables.

Avoid Repeated Allocations: Instead of repeatedly allocating and deallocating memory, consider using a memory pool or managing a free list to recycle memory blocks efficiently.

Align Data Properly: Proper alignment can lead to better performance, as many processors perform optimally when data structures align with their word sizes.

By understanding memory organization, effective use of addressing modes, and the careful management of stack and dynamic memory, assembly programmers can create highly efficient programs. The control afforded by assembly language allows developers to exploit system resources fully, paving the way for high- performance applications.

Understanding RAM, Stack, and Heap in Low-Level Programming

Among the critical components of memory are Random Access Memory (RAM), the stack, and the heap. Together, these elements dictate how data is stored, accessed, and manipulated during program execution. This chapter aims to demystify these components and illustrate their functionality within the context of assembly programming.

1. Random Access Memory (RAM)

RAM is a type of volatile memory used by computers to store data that is actively being worked on. It provides fast read and write access, making it essential for the efficient functioning of CPUs. When a program is executed, it is loaded from secondary storage (like hard drives) into RAM, allowing the CPU to access instructions and data quickly.

Characteristics of RAM

Volatility: Data in RAM is temporary and lost when the system is powered off.

Speed: RAM offers quick access times compared to other storage options, making it suitable for active processes.

Capacity: The amount of RAM in a system can vary widely, affecting the performance and multitasking capabilities of applications.

2. The Stack

The stack is a special region of RAM used for managing function calls and local variables. It operates in a Last In, First Out (LIFO) manner, meaning that the last item added to the stack is the first one to be removed.

Characteristics of the Stack

Functionality: When a function is called, a new stack frame is created containing its local variables, parameters, and return address. This organization ensures that after the function completes its execution, control can return to the exact point in the program from which it was called.

Memory Allocation: Stack allocation is managed automatically, with space being allocated and deallocated as functions are called and return.

Limitations: The stack has a fixed size, and excessive use, such as deep recursion, can lead to stack overflow, causing the program to crash.

Stack Operations in Assembly

In assembly, operations on the stack are typically handled using specific instructions. For instance:

PUSH: Place a value onto the stack.

POP: Remove a value from the stack.

CALL: Invoke a function and push its return address onto the stack.

RET: Return from a function, popping the return address off the stack. Here's a simple assembly code snippet demonstrating stack usage:

```assembly
assembly section .text global _start


_start:

push    5       ; Push the value 5 onto the stack

push    10      ; Push the value 10 onto the stack

call    my_function ; Call my_function
add     esp, 8 ; Clean up the stack (2 values popped)
```

```
my_function:

pop     eax    ; Pop the top value into eax pop    ebx    ;
Pop the next value into ebx

; Perform operations on eax and ebx ret
```
` ` `

3. The Heap

The heap is another segment of RAM, but it is used for dynamic memory allocation. Unlike the stack, where memory is allocated in a fixed order, the heap allows for more flexible memory management.

Characteristics of the Heap

Dynamic Allocation: Memory in the heap can be allocated and freed at any point during program execution, providing significant flexibility.

Management: Unlike the stack, the program must manually manage memory, leading to possibilities of fragmentation and memory leaks if not handled appropriately.

Size: The heap is generally larger than the stack and can grow in size as needed, but it is also more prone to performance hits due to the overhead of managing dynamic allocations.

Heap Operations in Assembly

In assembly programming, managing memory on the heap typically involves using system calls or library functions to request and release memory. For example, functions like `malloc` (to allocate memory) and

`free` (to release memory) in C can be invoked from

71

assembly.

Here's an example of how one might allocate memory on the heap using assembly:

```assembly
```assembly section .text global _start

_start:
; Allocate memory for 100 bytes

mov eax, 45      ; Syscall number for brk (in Linux)
xor ebx, ebx  ; Start from 0

int 0x80      ; Call the kernel

; Assume ebx now holds the new brk position

; Free memory (using brk to reset)

; This is just a crude example; heap management requires proper implementation.


; Clean up and exit

mov eax, 1    ; Syscall number for exit xor ebx, ebx      ;
Return code 0

int 0x80
```
```

4. Comparison of Stack and Heap

While both the stack and heap are used for managing memory, they serve different purposes and exhibit different behaviors:

| Feature | Stack | Heap |
|----------------|------------------------------| | |

Allocation	Automatic (LIFO)	Manual	
Size	Fixed	Dynamic	
Access Time	Fast	Slower due to management overhead	
Scope	Local to function	Global or shared across functions	
Fragmentation	No fragmentation	Can become fragmented	

Understanding RAM, the stack, and the heap is integral to mastering low-level programming in assembly language. By navigating these memory structures, programmers can write efficient, high-performance code while managing resources adeptly.

Addressing Modes and How Data Is Accessed in Memory

This chapter delves into addressing modes—various techniques used to access operands in assembly programming. By exploring these modes, you will gain a deeper insight into memory management and the efficient execution of machine-level instructions.

1. The Concept of Memory Access

Before we discuss addressing modes, it's critical to understand how data is organized in memory. Memory is typically structured as a contiguous array of storage locations, each identified by an address. In assembly programming, operations frequently involve fetching data from memory, processing it, and storing results back to specific memory locations.

Assembly instructions often work with operands that can be immediate values, register contents, or values stored in memory. The method of specifying where to find these operands is determined by the addressing mode.

2. Addressing Modes: An Overview

Addressing modes define the rules and techniques for locating the operands required by an instruction. The choice of addressing mode can significantly affect the efficiency and flexibility of the code. Below, we outline some of the most common addressing modes utilized in assembly programming.

2.1. Immediate Addressing Mode

In immediate addressing mode, the operand is a constant embedded directly within the instruction. This mode is straightforward and often used for initializing values.

Example:

```assembly
MOV AX, 5 ; Load the immediate value 5 into the AX register
```

2.2. Register Addressing Mode

Register addressing mode uses the operand stored in a CPU register. This mode is fast since accessing registers is quicker than fetching values from memory.

Example:

```assembly
```

MOV BX, AX ; Copy the contents of AX register into the BX register
```

### 2.3. Direct Addressing Mode

Direct addressing mode specifies the exact memory address of the operand. The instruction directly tells the CPU where to find the data.

**Example:**

```assembly
MOV AL, [1000h] ; Move the byte at memory location 1000h into AL register
```

2.4. Indirect Addressing Mode

In indirect addressing mode, the instruction specifies a register that contains the address of the operand rather than the operand itself. This allows for more flexible access patterns, such as accessing arrays or structures.

Example:

```assembly
MOV AX, [BX] ; Move the value stored at the address in register BX into AX
```

2.5. Indexed Addressing Mode

Indexed addressing mode uses a base address plus an offset to determine the effective address of the operand.
```

This mode is particularly useful for accessing array elements.

Example:

```assembly
MOV AX, [SI + 0x03] ; Move the value at the address of SI plus an offset of 3 into AX
```

2.6. Base-Offset Addressing Mode

This variant of indexed addressing combines a base register with a displacement to compute the effective address. It's commonly used for accessing structure members.

Example:

```assembly
MOV AX, [BX + SI] ; Move the value located at the address calculated by BX plus SI into AX
```

2.7. Relative Addressing Mode

Relative addressing mode is often utilized in branch instructions. The operand's address is determined by adding a constant value (signed offset) to the program counter (PC).

Example:

```assembly
JNZ Label ; Jump to Label if the zero flag is not set, where Label's address is calculated relative to the current
```

position
```

## 3. The Importance of Addressing Modes

Understanding addressing modes is vital for writing efficient assembly programs. Different modes provide various ways to optimize memory access, resulting in improved execution speed and reduced instruction count. Furthermore, the choice of addressing mode will affect how easily a programmer can manage data structures, control flows, and manipulate complex data types.

When writing assembly code, developers often must choose the most appropriate addressing mode for a particular task. This decision can impact the overall efficiency of the program and determine how easily the code can be maintained and extended in the future.

We explored the different addressing modes available in assembly programming and the corresponding methods for accessing data in memory. As assembly programmers, understanding how to leverage these addressing modes effectively can lead to highly efficient code that optimally interacts with system memory.
```

Chapter 6: Working with Arithmetic and Logical Operations

In this chapter, we will delve into the fundamental arithmetic and logical operations available in assembly programming. Understanding these operations is critical not only for performing calculations but also for manipulating data at a low level, which is pivotal in system programming, embedded systems, and performance-critical applications.

6.1 Basics of Arithmetic Operations

Arithmetic operations in assembly can be categorized into several basic functions: addition, subtraction, multiplication, and division. Each of these operations has specific instructions and requirements based on the architecture of the processor you are working on (e.g., x86, ARM).

6.1.1 Addition

In assembly languages like x86, the `ADD` instruction is utilized to add two operands. The result is stored in the destination operand.

Example:

```asm
MOV AX, 5   ; Move the value 5 into register AX

ADD AX, 3   ; Add 3 to the value in AX, resulting in AX = 8
```

6.1.2 Subtraction

The `SUB` instruction functions similarly to `ADD`. It subtracts the second operand from the first and stores the result in the first operand.

Example:

```asm
MOV BX, 10        ; Move the value 10 into register BX
SUB BX, 7     ; Subtract 7 from BX, resulting in BX = 3
```

6.1.3 Multiplication

In x86 assembly, multiplication can be accomplished using the `MUL` (for unsigned numbers) or `IMUL` (for signed numbers) instructions. The result is stored in a specific register pair.

Example:

```asm
MOV AX, 4   ; Load AX with 4 MOV BX, 3      ; Load BX with 3

MUL BX      ; Multiply AX by BX, the result (12) is stored in AX
```

6.1.4 Division

Division is performed using the `DIV` (unsigned) and `IDIV` (signed) instructions. These instructions require specific preparation of the dividend and set the quotient and remainder in different registers.

Example:

```asm
MOV AX, 20        ; Load AX with 20 (dividend) MOV BL, 4  ; Load BL with 4 (divisor)

DIV BL      ; Divide AX by BL, quotient in AL, remainder in AH
```

6.2 Understanding Logical Operations

Logical operations include AND, OR, NOT, and XOR, and are used for bit-level manipulation, which is crucial in system-level programming tasks such as flags, masks, and control structures.

6.2.1 AND Operation

The `AND` instruction performs a bitwise AND operation between two operands. The result is stored in the destination operand.

Example:

```asm
MOV AL, 0x0F  ; Load AL with 00001111 MOV BL, 0xF0 ; Load BL with 11110000

AND AL, BL ; AL = 00000000 (since 0x0F AND 0xF0 = 0)
```

6.2.2 OR Operation

The `OR` operation combines the bits of two operands, resulting in a set bit if either of the operand bits are set.

Example:

80

```asm
MOV AL, 0x0F  ; Load AL with 00001111
OR AL, 0xF0 ; AL = 11111111 (0x0F OR 0xF0 = 0xFF)
```

6.2.3 NOT Operation

The `NOT` instruction inverts all bits of its operand. This is a unary operation.

Example:

```asm
MOV AL, 0x0F  ; Load AL with 00001111
NOT AL        ; AL = 11110000 (the bitwise NOT of 0x0F)
```

6.2.4 XOR Operation

The `XOR` instruction performs a bitwise exclusive OR operation. It sets each bit to 1 if the corresponding bits of both operands are different.

Example:

```asm
MOV AL, 5  ; Load AL with 00000101 MOV BL, 3  ; Load BL with 00000011 XOR AL, BL  ; AL = 6 (0110)
```

6.3 Practical Applications of Arithmetic and Logical Operations ### 6.3.1 Counting and Indexing

Arithmetic operations are often used in loops and

counters. For example, incrementing values, calculating array indices, or managing file offsets.

6.3.2 Bit Masks

Logical operations, particularly AND, OR, and NOT, are frequently used in situations requiring bit manipulation, such as setting, clearing, or toggling specific bits within a register.

6.3.3 Control Flow

Understanding how to manipulate values using logical and arithmetic operations is key to controlling flow in programming, especially in conditions and loops.

The ability to perform arithmetic and logical operations efficiently is fundamental to successful assembly programming. As demonstrated, assembly language offers direct control over hardware through these operations, making it invaluable in various programming tasks, from performance optimization to system-level coding.

Performing Basic Arithmetic: Addition, Subtraction, Multiplication, and Division

This chapter will explore how to perform these basic arithmetic operations in assembly language, focusing on the general concepts that can stretch across various assembly dialects, including x86 and ARM.

The Basics of Assembly Arithmetic

Before diving into specific operations, it's essential to understand how data is represented in assembly programming. Typically, integers can be represented using binary values, which the CPU processes as individual bits. The basic arithmetic operations manipulate these binary values to perform calculations.

Data Types

Assembly language typically supports various data types, including:

Byte: 8 bits

Word: 16 bits (in x86)

Double Word (DWORD): 32 bits

Quad Word (QWORD): 64 bits

Knowing how to handle these data types is crucial since operations may vary based on the size of the data being manipulated.

Addition

Instruction Overview

In assembly language, the addition operation is commonly performed using the `ADD` instruction. The general syntax for using the `ADD` instruction is:

```
ADD destination, source
```

Here, the value from `source` is added to `destination`, and the result is stored in `destination`. ### Example: Adding Two Numbers

Let's look at an example where we add two integers. Assume we want to add the numbers stored in registers

`EAX` and `EBX` in x86 assembly.

```assembly
section .data
num1 db 10   ; Define byte data
num2 db 20   ; Define another byte data
section .text global _start
```

_start:

```
mov al, [num1]  ; Load num1 into AL register add al, [num2]  ; Add num2 to AL
; Result now in AL
```

Setting Flags

When performing addition, the CPU sets status flags (such as the Zero Flag (ZF) and Carry Flag (CF)) to indicate the outcome of the operation.

Subtraction

Instruction Overview

Subtraction in assembly can be carried out using the `SUB` instruction. Similar to addition, its syntax is:

```

SUB destination, source
```

Example: Subtracting Two Numbers

Here's an example of subtraction, where we subtract one register value from another.

84

```assembly
section .data
num1 db 20
num2 db 10

section .text global _start
_start:

mov al, [num1]  ; Load num1 into AL  sub al, [num2]  ; Subtract num2 from AL

; Result now in AL
```

Multiplication

Instruction Overview

For multiplication, the `MUL` instruction is used for unsigned multiplication, and `IMUL` is used for signed multiplication. The key point to remember is that multiplication affects registers in a particular way:

For `MUL`: If you multiply two bytes, the result goes into AX; if you multiply two words, the result goes into DX:AX.

For `IMUL`: The same applies but takes into consideration the sign of the operands. ### Example: Multiplying Two Numbers

Here's an example of multiplying values in x86 assembly:

```assembly
section .data num1 db 5
num2 db 6

section .text global _start
```

```
_start:
mov al, [num1]  ; Load num1 into AL
mul byte [num2] ; Multiply AL by num2 (result in AX)
; Result now in AX
```

Overflow Handling

It's crucial to handle the possibility of overload in multiplication; for instance, if the result exceeds the storage capabilities of the destination register.

Division

Instruction Overview

Division is performed using the `DIV` (unsigned) or `IDIV` (signed) instructions. It is important to note that the dividend (the number being divided) should be stored in the AX register (or DX:AX for larger values), while the divisor is specified in the instruction.

Example: Dividing Two Numbers Here's how to perform a division operation:

```
assembly section .data
num1 db 20
num2 db 5
section .text global _start
_start:
mov al, [num1] ; Load num1 into AL xor ah, ah; Clear AH
for division div byte [num2] ; Divide AL by num2
; Quotient in AL, Remainder in AH
```

```
` ` `
```

Handling Division by Zero

It's vital to include checks for division by zero, as it will cause a runtime error. This can be handled in your code by checking if the divisor is zero before performing the operation.

By understanding how addition, subtraction, multiplication, and division work at this low level, programmers can harness the full power of the hardware they are programming for, enabling the development of optimized algorithms and applications.

Logical Operations and Bitwise Manipulation

Logical operations are fundamental in programming, allowing developers to make decisions based on certain conditions. In assembly language, logical operations work on binary values, facilitating low-level data handling and control flow. This chapter will explore the primary logical operations available in assembly programming, how they function, and their applications in coding.

1.1 Types of Logical Operations

Assembly language provides several logical operations, including:

AND

OR

NOT

XOR (Exclusive OR)

Each of these operations performs a different function and can be combined with bitwise manipulation techniques to provide powerful control over data.

1.2 The AND Operation

The AND operation takes two binary operands and performs a bitwise comparison. For each bit, the result is 1 if both bits are 1; otherwise, the result is 0. The syntax in x86 assembly might look like this:

```assembly
AND destination, source
```

Example:

Consider the following example:

```assembly
MOV AL, 10101010b ; Load AL register with 10101010
MOV BL, 11001100b ; Load BL register with 11001100
AND AL, BL ; Perform AND operation
```

The result in AL would be `10001000`, as only the third and the eighth bits from the right are 1 in both operands.

1.3 The OR Operation

The OR operation also takes two binary operands but returns 1 if at least one of the bits is 1.

```assembly
OR destination, source
```

Example:

```assembly
MOV AL, 10101010b ; Load AL register with 10101010
MOV BL, 11001100b ; Load BL register with 11001100 OR
AL, BL ; Perform OR operation
```

The result in AL would be `11101110`, as bits will be set to 1 wherever at least one operand has a 1 in that position.

1.4 The NOT Operation

The NOT operation is a unary operation that inverts each bit of its operand.

```assembly NOT destination
```

Example:

```assembly
MOV AL, 10101010b ; Load AL register with 10101010
NOT AL ; Perform NOT operation
```

The result in AL would be `01010101`, effectively flipping all bits. ### 1.5 The XOR Operation

The XOR operation returns 1 only when the bits are different.

```assembly
XOR destination, source
```

```
```

Example:

```assembly
```

MOV AL, 10101010b ; Load AL register with 10101010
MOV BL, 11001100b ; Load BL register with 11001100
XOR AL, BL ; Perform XOR operation

```
```

The result in AL would be `01100110`, as only the bits that differ between the operands are set to 1. ## Introduction to Bitwise Manipulation

Bitwise manipulation involves updating individual bits within a binary number, allowing precise control over data representation and encoding. In assembly language, bitwise manipulation is essential for tasks such as setting flags, masking bits, and manipulating individual components of multi-bit data.

2.1 Shifting Bits

Shifting operations can alter the position of bits within a binary number, which can be particularly useful for multiplication or division by powers of two.

Left Shift (SHL): Moves bits to the left, filling with zeros. Each shift left effectively multiplies the number by 2.

```assembly
```

SHL destination, count

```
```

Right Shift (SHR): Moves bits to the right, filling with the sign bit (for signed numbers) or zeros. Each shift right effectively divides the number by 2.

```assembly
SHR destination, count
```

Example of Shifting

```assembly
MOV AL, 00000001b ; Load AL with 1
SHL AL, 1 ; Shift left
```

After this operation, AL will contain `00000010` (2 in decimal). ### 2.2 Masking Bits

Masking involves using bitwise operations with a predefined pattern to isolate or modify specific bits within a byte or larger data types. This is commonly done with AND, OR, and XOR operations.

For example, to set the 3rd bit of a byte, you could use:

```assembly
MOV AL, 00000000b ; Load AL
OR AL, 00000100b ; Set the 3rd bit
```

To clear the 3rd bit, you would use a mask with AND:

```assembly
MOV AL, 00000111b ; Load AL
```

```
AND AL, 11111011b  ; Clear the 3rd bit
```
\ \ \

Applications of Logical Operations and Bitwise Manipulation ### 3.1 Control Structures

Logical operations form the basis of control structures such as conditional jumps. For example, a programmer might use the AND operation to determine if multiple conditions are true before proceeding to a specific segment of code.

3.2 Flags and Status Registers

Manipulating status registers often requires using bitwise operations to set, clear, or toggle specific flags. This is common in systems programming, where efficient control over hardware states is necessary.

3.3 Data Compression and Encryption

Bitwise manipulation techniques play a critical role in data compression algorithms and cryptographic operations.

Logical operations and bitwise manipulation in assembly language provide powerful tools for developers to interact directly with the underlying hardware. Understanding these operations is crucial to optimizing performance and accomplishing complex computational tasks at the bit level.

Chapter 7: Control Flow and Decision Making

This is especially true in assembly programming, where programmers work closely with the hardware and must dictate the sequence of operations at a low level. Unlike high-level languages that offer built-in constructs for control flow such as loops and conditionals, assembly language requires a more manual approach. This chapter explores the various mechanisms available for decision-making and flow control in assembly programming.

7.1 Understanding Control Flow

Control flow refers to the order in which individual statements, instructions, or function calls are executed or evaluated in a program. In assembly language, control flow is generally achieved through a combination of jumps, loops, and conditional branching. The primary flow control constructs in assembly can be categorized into:

Unconditional Jumps

Conditional Jumps

Loops

7.1.1 Unconditional Jumps

Unconditional jumps are used to alter the flow by jumping to a specific label or memory address, regardless of any conditions. The most common instruction for an unconditional jump is `JMP`.

Example:

```assembly
start:
```

```
; Some operations
JMP start ; Infinite loop
```

In this example, the program will continually jump back to the label `start`, creating an infinite loop. ### 7.1.2 Conditional Jumps

Conditional jumps involve checking the status of flags in the processor's status register and making branching decisions based on those flags. Common conditions check for equality (`JE` - Jump if Equal), inequality (`JNE` - Jump if Not Equal), greater than (`JG` - Jump if Greater), and less than (`JL` - Jump if Less).

Example:

```assembly
mov eax, 5
cmp eax, 10
jl less_than ; Jump to 'less_than' if eax is less than 10
; Execute if not less than mov ebx, 1
less_than:
; Execute if less than 10
```

In this segment, if `eax` is less than 10, the program will jump to the `less_than` label to execute associated instructions. Otherwise, it will continue to the next block of code.

7.1.3 Loops

Loops are fundamental constructs for repeating a

sequence of instructions. These can be implemented through conditional jumps together with counters or conditional checks.

Example:

```assembly
mov ecx, 5 ; Loop counter loop_start:
; Some operations
dec ecx ; Decrement counter
jnz loop_start ; Jump back if ecx is not zero
```

In this example, the loop continues executing the instructions until `ecx` reaches zero. The `JNZ` instruction (Jump if Not Zero) serves as the condition for looping.

7.2 Decision-Making Constructs

Decision-making in assembly programming often requires combining the jump instructions with comparisons to make divergent paths based on runtime conditions. This section will expand on how to effectively use comparisons and branches for making decisions.

7.2.1 Comparison Instructions

Before making decisions, we need to compare values. The `CMP` instruction subtracts one value from another but does not store the result; instead, it sets the processor flags based on the outcome.

For example, using `CMP` in conjunction with a conditional jump can help decide the path of execution:

95

```assembly
mov eax, 5
mov ebx, 5 cmp eax, ebx
je equal_case ; Jump to equal_case if eax == ebx
; Not equal case
equal_case:
; Equal branch executed
```

7.2.2 Nested Decision Making

Complex decision making may involve nested conditional branches, allowing multiple layers of decision logic. This enables the programmer to handle various scenarios by systematically comparing conditions.

Example:

```assembly
mov eax, 2 ; Sample value cmp eax, 1
je case_one cmp eax, 2 je case_two
jmp default_case
case_one:
; Handle case one jmp end_case
case_two:
; Handle case two jmp end_case
default_case:
; Handle default case
end_case:
```

```
```

In this code, multiple conditions are evaluated, and based on the value of `eax`, the program directs execution to the appropriate case.

7.3 Practical Applications

Control flow and decision-making in assembly programming have numerous practical applications. Understanding these concepts is vital for tasks in systems programming, real-time systems, and low-level application development.

7.3.1 System Programming

In operating systems and embedded systems, control flow is crucial for process management, interrupt handling, and resource allocation. Assembly language allows precise control over these low-level functions.

7.3.2 Performance Optimization

By using efficient control flow and decision-making constructs, programmers can optimize performance-critical code, reducing cycles and improving speed.

Control flow and decision-making are fundamental aspects of assembly programming, giving programmers the tools necessary to dictate how programs behave based on runtime conditions. Mastery of these constructs not only enhances the ability to manipulate hardware efficiently but also lays a strong foundation for understanding more complex programming paradigms in higher-level languages.

Implementing Conditional Statements: Jumps and Comparisons

Conditional statements are a fundamental aspect of programming, allowing for decision-making based on specific criteria. In high-level programming languages, these constructs are often represented using straightforward syntax, such as `if`, `else`, and `switch`. However, low-level assembly language operates quite differently. Here, we will explore how conditional statements are implemented using jumps and comparisons, providing a foundational understanding of control flow in assembly programming.

Understanding Assembly Language Basics

Before diving into conditional statements, it is crucial to grasp some fundamental concepts of assembly language:

Machine Language vs. Assembly Language: Assembly language is a human-readable representation of machine language. Each assembly instruction corresponds directly to a machine code instruction that the computer's CPU can execute.

Registers and Memory: Assembly programming primarily involves operations on registers (small, fast storage locations within the CPU) and memory (larger storage accessible by the CPU).

Instruction Set Architecture (ISA): Each CPU architecture (like x86, ARM, MIPS) has its specific instruction set, which includes a variety of operations, including arithmetic, logical, data movement, and control flow instructions.

The Role of Comparison and Jump Instructions

In assembly programming, conditional execution is achieved through a combination of comparison and jump instructions.

Comparison Instructions

Comparison instructions are used to evaluate the relationship between two operands. This is typically done using specific flags that are set based on the outcome of the comparison. Common comparison instructions include:

CMP (Compare): Subtracts one value from another and sets the CPU flags accordingly. It does not store the result; it only affects the flags.

TEST: Performs a bitwise AND between two values and sets the flags based on the result. The flags commonly used in conditional statements are:

Zero Flag (ZF): Set if the result of the comparison is zero.

Sign Flag (SF): Set if the result is negative.

Carry Flag (CF): Set if there was a borrow in an unsigned comparison. ### Jump Instructions

Jump instructions alter the flow of execution depending on the state of flags set by previous comparisons. There are two types of jumps:

Unconditional Jumps: These instructions cause the program to jump to a specified address or label regardless of the conditions. An example is the `JMP` instruction.

Conditional Jumps: These instructions only perform

the jump if a specified condition is met. Examples include:

JE (Jump if Equal): Jumps if ZF is set.

JNE (Jump if Not Equal): Jumps if ZF is clear.

JG (Jump if Greater): Jumps if ZF is clear and SF equals OF (overflow flag).

JL (Jump if Less): Jumps if SF is not equal to OF. ## Implementing Conditional Statements

With a solid understanding of comparison and jump instructions, we can implement conditional statements in assembly language.

Example: Implementing an IF Statement

Let's illustrate the implementation of a simple `if` statement in assembly. The pseudocode is as follows:

```plaintext if (x > y) { z = x + y;
}
```

Here's how this could be translated into x86 assembly language:

```assembly section .data
x dd 5 ; Define x and y
y dd 3
z dd 0 ; Define z
section .text global _start
_start:
; Load x and y into registers for comparison mov eax, [x]
```

```asm
                    ; Load x into eax
mov ebx, [y]  ; Load y into ebx


; Compare x and y

cmp eax, ebx ; Compare x and y

jle .end_if     ; Jump to end_if if x <= y (ZF=1 or SF!=OF)

; If x > y, perform z = x + y

add eax, ebx  ; EAX now holds x + y mov [z], eax          ;
Store the result in z

.end_if:

; Program continues here (end of the IF statement)

; More code can go here

; Exit program

mov eax, 1     ; sys_exit system call number xor ebx, ebx
        ; Return code 0

int 0x80       ; Call kernel
```

Breaking Down the Example

Data Declaration: The values for `x`, `y`, and `z` are defined in the `.data` section.

Load Values: The values of `x` and `y` are loaded into registers `eax` and `ebx`, respectively.

Comparison: The `cmp` instruction compares the two values. The subsequent `jle` instruction checks if `x` is less than or equal to `y`. If true, control jumps to the label

`.end_if`, skipping the addition operation.

Execution of True Block: If `x` is greater than `y`, the program continues to add the two values and store the result in `z`.

Program Exit: Finally, the program exits cleanly.

Understanding how to manipulate flags and utilize jumps allows programmers to create complex decision- making processes at a low level. Mastery of these concepts not only enhances coding skills in assembly but also deepens one's understanding of how higher-level languages translate into machine operations.

Loops in Assembly: Loop, JMP, and Conditional Branching

This is essential for implementing repetitive tasks and making decisions based on conditions. In this chapter, we will delve into loops, unconditional jumps, and conditional branching, exploring how they can be employed to create efficient and effective programs in assembly language.

Understanding Control Flow

Assembly language operates closely with the hardware architecture of a computer, translating directly to machine code. As a result, control flow is often managed through the use of specific instructions that dictate the routing of program execution. Loops, jumps, and branches are the chief mechanisms for achieving non- linear execution paths, allowing developers to create dynamic and responsive programs.

Loops

A loop is a fundamental concept in programming where a set of instructions is executed repeatedly until a specific condition is met. In assembly language, loops are typically implemented through a combination of jump instructions and condition checking.

Types of Loops

Count-Controlled Loops: These loops iterate a predetermined number of times. For instance, if you want to execute a block of code ten times, you would decrease a counter from ten to zero on each iteration.

Condition-Controlled Loops: These loops continue executing until a specific condition changes. For example, a loop can keep running until a particular variable reaches a specified value.

Implementing a Loop

Let's look at a simple example of a count-controlled loop in x86 assembly. This code snippet counts from 10 down to 0 and prints each number:

```assembly
section .data
msg db "Count: %d", 10, 0

section .bss num resb 4

section .text extern printf global _start
_start:
mov ecx, 10   ; Initialize counter to 10
loop_start:
push ecx      ; Save counter on stack
```

```assembly
    push num      ; Prepare to push number for printing

    mov eax, ecx  ; Move counter to eax
    push eax      ; Push value to stack as an argument push
    msg           ; Push message format
    call printf   ; Call printf
    add esp, 12   ; Clean up stack (3 pushes * 4 bytes each)
    pop ecx       ; Restore counter from stack
    loop loop_start  ; Decrement ecx and loop if ecx != 0
; Exit Program
    mov eax, 1    ; syscall for exit xor ebx, ebx    ; return 0
    int 0x80
```

In this example, the `loop` instruction simplifies the iteration process by automatically decrementing the

`ecx` register and jumping back to the specified label if `ecx` is not zero. This provides a clean way to implement a loop.

JMP Instruction

The `JMP` (Jump) instruction is used to unconditionally transfer control to another location in the program. This can be used for a variety of purposes including creating loops, branching, or implementing simple control flow constructs.

Example of an unconditional jump:

```assembly
```

104

```
_start:

jmp label     ; Jump to label

label:

; Code to execute after jump
```
` ` `

Conditional Branching

Conditional branching allows the program to make decisions based on the content of registers or comparisons between different values. Assembly language provides several instructions for branching, including `JE` (Jump if Equal), `JNE` (Jump if Not Equal), `JG` (Jump if Greater), and `JL` (Jump if Less).

Decision-Making Example

Let's consider an example where we compare two numbers and jump to different code blocks based on which number is larger:

` ` `assembly section .text

global _start

_start:

mov eax, 5   ; First number mov ebx, 10   ;   Second number

cmp eax, ebx ; Compare eax with ebx jg first_larger ; Jump if eax > ebx

jl second_larger ; Jump if eax < ebx

equal:

```
; Code if numbers are equal jmp end      ; Jump to end
first_larger:
; Code if the first number is larger jmp end      ; Jump to
end
second_larger:
; Code if the second number is larger
end:
; Exit Program
mov eax, 1    ; syscall for exit xor ebx, ebx        ; return 0
int 0x80
```
` ` `

In this example, the `CMP` instruction is used to compare `eax` and `ebx`. Depending on the comparison result, the program branches to the appropriate label using conditional jump instructions.

By combining these constructs, programmers can create complex and dynamic logical structures. Understanding these mechanisms is essential for mastering assembly programming, offering tight control over hardware and optimizing performance.

Chapter 8: Working with Functions and Procedures

This chapter delves into the role of functions and procedures in assembly programming, discussing their definitions, structures, calling conventions, and practical applications.

8.1 Understanding Functions and Procedures

In the context of programming, a **function** is a block of code designed to perform a specific task and can return a value, while a **procedure** is similar but does not return a value. Both functions and procedures improve the readability and manageability of the code by promoting reusability and separation of concerns.

In assembly language, functions and procedures are typically defined using labels, with the operations within them being executed sequentially. While the terminology may vary between languages, the underlying principles remain the same.

8.2 Defining Functions and Procedures in Assembly
8.2.1 General Structure

The general structure of a function in assembly language consists of the following parts:

Function/Procedure Label: This identifier marks the entry point of the function.

Prologue: This part often contains code for setting up the stack frame, saving registers, and allocating local variables.

Body: The main operations or computations performed by the function.

Epilogue: This section prepares for the function's exit, restoring registers and stack pointers.

Return Statement: An instruction that directs the flow back to the calling function. ### Example of a Simple Function

Here is a simple example in x86 assembly language that defines a function to add two integers:

```assembly
section .text global _start

_start:

; Call the add function with arguments mov eax, 5      ; first argument

mov ebx, 10         ; second argument call add;  call  the add function

; Result is now in eax

; Exit program

mov eax, 1    ; syscall: exit int 0x80

add:

; Prologue

push ebp      ; save base pointer

mov ebp, esp ; set stack frame

; Body

mov eax, [ebp+8]  ; get the first argument add eax, [ebp+12] ; add the second argument

; Epilogue
```

```
pop ebp              ; restore base pointer ret    ; return to
caller
```

8.3 Calling Conventions

Calling conventions outline how functions receive parameters from the caller and how they return results. Different platforms and architectures may have different calling conventions, but several key elements are generally involved:

Parameter Passing: Parameters may be passed via the stack, registers, or a combination of both. For instance, in x86 calling conventions, the first few arguments are often passed in registers (like EAX, EBX, etc.), while additional arguments are pushed onto the stack.

Return Values: In many conventions, the return value of a function is placed in the EAX register.

Stack Management: The caller and callee must have a mutual understanding of who is responsible for stack cleanup. This is crucial for preventing stack corruption.

Example of a Calling Convention

Here's how the calling convention affects the previous addition function:

```assembly
section .text global _start

_start:

mov eax, 5

mov ebx, 10 call add
```

; EAX contains the sum

; Exit program mov eax, 1

int 0x80

add:

; Using registers to pass parameters add eax, ebx ; EAX = EAX + EBX ret

```
```

8.4 Local Variables and Stack Frames

When working with functions, you may want to use local variables. These variables can be stored in the stack frame—memory allocated for the function when it is called. Proper stack management is essential for avoiding data corruption and ensuring that local variables are properly isolated between function calls.

Allocating Local Variables

In our previous example, local variables can be allocated as follows:

```assembly
add:
```

push ebp   ; save the base pointer mov ebp, esp   ; set up stack frame

sub esp, 4   ; allocate space for one local variable

; Perform addition

mov eax, [ebp+8] ; first parameter

mov [ebp-4], eax ; store in local variable add eax, [ebp+12] ; second parameter mov eax, [ebp-4] ; retrieve

110

local variable

; Clean up

leave   ; equivalent to mov esp, ebp; pop ebp ret

```
```

8.5 Recursion

Functions can call themselves, which is known as recursion. This technique can simplify problems like calculating factorials or solving Fibonacci sequences. However, recursion requires careful management of the stack to prevent overflow.

Example of a Recursive Function

Here's a simple implementation of a recursive factorial function:

```assembly
factorial:
; Prologue push ebp mov ebp, esp

; Base case

cmp dword [ebp+8], 1 jle .base_case

; Recursive case

mov eax, [ebp+8]            ; n dec eax    ; n - 1

push eax                ; push n - 1 to stack  call factorial
      ; call factorial(n - 1) pop ebx        ;  restore  n  -  1
from stack

imul eax, ebx ; factorial(n) = n * factorial(n - 1) pop ebp

ret

.base_case:
```

```
mov eax, 1    ; return 1 for n <= 1 pop ebp
ret
```
\ \ \

Functions and procedures are fundamental aspects of assembly programming that enhance the structure and maintainability of code. Understanding how to define, call, and manage these constructs—along with adhering to calling conventions and properly handling local variables—empowers developers to write efficient and modular programs.

Calling and Defining Procedures in Assembly

This chapter delves into the concepts of defining and calling procedures in assembly language, providing a framework to streamline complex tasks, manage resources, and improve program readability.

1. Understanding Procedures

A procedure is a self-contained block of code designed to perform a specific operation. It allows programmers to break their applications into smaller, manageable pieces, which can be called multiple times throughout the program. Procedures in assembly language may take parameters, return values, and interact with both local and global variables.

1.1 The Purpose of Procedures

The use of procedures provides several advantages:

Code Reusability: Once defined, a procedure can be called whenever needed, minimizing redundancy.

Improved Readability: Procedures can encapsulate specific functionalities, making the main program flow easier to understand.

Modular Programming: Procedures allow for a modular approach, where programs can be developed in segments and then integrated.

Ease of Maintenance: Changes can be made in one place (the procedure) rather than multiple locations within the code.

2. Defining a Procedure

In assembly language, a procedure is defined using specific directives that inform the assembler where the procedure starts and ends. The general format for defining a procedure can vary between different assembly languages (for example, NASM, MASM, etc.), but the underlying concepts are often similar.

2.1 Basic Procedure Syntax

Here's an example of a simple procedure definition in NASM syntax:

``` assembly section .text global _start

_start:

; Call the add_numbers procedure mov eax, 5  ;      First parameter mov ebx, 10            ; Second parameter

call add_numbers   ; Call the procedure

; Exit the program

mov eax, 1    ; syscall number for exit xor ebx, ebx       ; exit code 0
```

```
int 0x80
```

; Define the add_numbers procedure add_numbers:

; Parameters are in eax and ebx

```
add eax, ebx  ; Perform addition


ret     ; Return to the caller
```
` ` `

In this example:

The procedure `add_numbers` takes two parameters passed in registers `eax` and `ebx`.

When the `call` instruction is invoked, control is transferred to the `add_numbers` procedure where the addition is performed.

The `ret` instruction is used to return control back to the instruction following the `call`. ### 2.2 Parameters and Local Variables

Procedures can accept parameters, which can be passed via registers, the stack, or memory. In our previous example, we used registers. Here's how parameters can also be passed via the stack:

` ` `assembly add_numbers:

```
push ebp     ; Save the base pointer  mov ebp, esp
        ; Set a new base pointer mov eax, [ebp + 8]
        ; Get the first parameter
```

```
mov ebx, [ebp + 12] ; Get the second parameter add eax,
ebx     ; Perform addition
```

```
pop ebp              ; Restore the base pointer ret      ;
Return to the caller
```
` ` `

In this version, the parameters are pushed onto the stack before the `call` instruction, and accessed within the procedure by using the base pointer `ebp`.

3. Calling a Procedure

Calling a procedure involves using the `call` instruction, which changes the control flow of a program to the specified procedure. When a procedure is called, the current execution context (instruction pointer) is pushed onto the stack, allowing for a return point after the procedure's execution.

3.1 The Call Stack

The call stack is a fundamental part of procedure calls, allowing for nested calls and maintaining state. As procedures are called, the call stack grows, and when they return, this stack unwinds.

Pushing the Return Address: When `call` is executed, the address of the next instruction is pushed onto the stack.

Transfer of Control: Execution jumps to the procedure.

Returning from the Procedure: The `ret` instruction pops the return address and transfers control back.

3.2 Example of Calling a Nested Procedure

Let's look at an example where we have a general procedure that calls another nested procedure:

```assembly
section .text
global _start
_start:
call outer_procedure        ; Call first procedure
; Exit program mov eax, 1  xor ebx, ebx int 0x80
outer_procedure:
; Manages some initialization
call inner_procedure        ; Call nested procedure ret ;
Return to the caller
inner_procedure:
; Execute some task

ret     ; Return to outer_procedure
```

In this case, `outer_procedure` manages some tasks and delegates certain operations to `inner_procedure`. Control flow and the call stack handle the procedures' interconnections seamlessly.

4. Returning Values from Procedures

To return values from a procedure, the value is typically placed in a designated register before the `ret` instruction. Common conventions include using `eax` for return values.

```assembly
multiply_numbers:

mov eax, [esp + 4]   ; First parameter mov ebx, [esp + 8]
       ; Second parameter

mul ebx                ; EAX = EAX * EBX (Result in eax) ret
```

```
; Return to the caller
```
` ` `

By leveraging procedures, programmers can write cleaner, more organized programs that facilitate debugging, enhancement, and collaboration. Through understanding how to pass parameters, manage the call stack, and return values, developers can significantly enhance the functionality and readability of their assembly language projects.

Using the Stack for Function Calls and Parameter Passing

One of the central structures for this is the stack, a region of memory that operates on a Last-In-First-Out (LIFO) basis. This chapter delves into the usage of the stack for handling function calls and parameter passing, two critical aspects of assembly programming. By understanding how to manipulate the stack effectively, programmers can ensure that their applications execute correctly and efficiently.

The Role of the Stack

The stack serves multiple purposes in assembly programming, including:

Function Call Management: It keeps track of multiple function calls, which is crucial for nested or recursive functions.

Local Storage: It temporarily holds local variables, return addresses, and registers that need to be saved.

Parameter Passing: The stack provides a convenient way to pass parameters to functions.

Understanding the stack's structure and operations is vital for exploitative assembly programming practices. ## Basic Stack Operations

Before discussing function calls, let's recapitulate the fundamental operations of the stack:

Push: This operation adds an item to the top of the stack. In assembly language, this typically involves decrementing the stack pointer (SP) and saving the value at the new address.

Pop: This operation removes the item from the top of the stack and returns the stack pointer to its previous location. The value is retrieved from the address currently pointed to by SP, and SP is then incremented.

Stack Pointer: The stack pointer (often SP or ESP in x86 architecture) holds the address of the current top of the stack. The stack grows downwards in memory, meaning that pushing values decreases the stack pointer's value.

Function Calls in Assembly

When a function is called in an assembly program, several steps are taken that utilize the stack. Let's go through the typical function call process:

Push Return Address: When a function is called, the address of the next instruction (the return point) is pushed onto the stack. This allows the program to return to the correct location after the function completes.

Set Up the Stack Frame: This includes allocating

space on the stack for local variables and saving any registers that might be modified within the function.

Save Parameters: If the function requires parameters, these are either pushed onto the stack (depending on the calling convention) before the call or passed through registers.

Call the Function: The `CALL` instruction is used to jump to the function's code. The CPU now executes the function with the stacked return address in mind.

Return from Function: Once the function completes its task, it uses the `RET` instruction to pop the return address off the stack and jump back to that location.

Example of Function Call

Let's analyze a simple assembly example using NASM syntax.

```asm
```asm section .data

msg db 'Hello, World!', 0

section .text global _start

_start:

; Calling PrintMessage function

push msg     ; Push the message address as a parameter
call PrintMessage

add esp, 4     ; Clean up the stack after the call

; Exit program

mov eax, 1     ; syscall: exit xor ebx, ebx     ; status: 0

int 0x80
```
```

```
PrintMessage:
; Function to print the message
push ebp       ; Save the base pointer
mov ebp, esp ; Set the base pointer for this frame
mov eax, 4     ; syscall: write
mov ebx, 1     ; file descriptor: stdout
mov ecx, [ebp+8] ; Get the parameter (address of msg)
mov edx, 14   ; length of the message
int 0x80
pop ebp                ; Restore the base pointer ret       ;
Return to the caller
```

In this example, we see the function `PrintMessage` being called. The address of `msg` is passed on the stack, and after the function returns, we clean up the stack by adjusting the stack pointer.

Parameter Passing Conventions

Several conventions dictate how parameters are passed to functions, which can vary by architecture and programming conventions. Common methods include:

Stack-based Passing: Parameters are pushed onto the stack before the call. This method allows for variable-length parameters but can be inefficient due to additional overhead.

Register-based Passing: Some systems allow the use of registers to pass a fixed number of parameters, which can improve performance but limits the number of parameters passed.

Understanding the specific calling conventions used by the architecture in question is crucial for ensuring that function parameters are handled correctly.

Managing Local Variables

When using the stack for function calls, local variables can be allocated by adjusting the stack pointer at the beginning of the function:

```asm
PrintMessage:

push ebp mov ebp, esp

sub esp, 16    ; Allocate space for local variables (e.g., 16 bytes)

; Your logic here, possibly using the local space

leave  ; This is equivalent to moving esp back to ebp, popping ebp ret
```

By mastering stack operations and understanding function call conventions, programmers can write effective and efficient assembly code. This chapter sets a foundation upon which further concepts, such as recursive function calls and more complex parameter handling strategies, can be built.

Chapter 9: Handling Input and Output in Assembly

In this chapter, we will explore the various mechanisms available for managing I/O in assembly language, focusing on reading from and writing to different I/O channels.

9.1 Understanding I/O in Assembly Language

In the context of assembly language, I/O operations generally fall into two categories: **programmed I/O** and **interrupt-driven I/O**. Programmed I/O requires the CPU to actively wait for an I/O operation to complete, whereas interrupt-driven I/O allows the CPU to perform other tasks while waiting for an operation to complete, thereby improving efficiency.

9.1.1 Programmed I/O

Programmed I/O involves direct control over I/O operations by the CPU. In this method, the CPU checks the status of the I/O device before reading from or writing to it. This can be particularly useful in simpler systems or when performing low-level operations.

9.1.2 Interrupt-Driven I/O

In contrast, interrupt-driven I/O allows devices to signal the CPU when they are ready for data transfer. This technique is more efficient, as it frees up the CPU to perform other tasks instead of polling the I/O devices continuously.

9.2 Input/Output Interfaces in Assembly

Different platforms provide distinct methods for handling I/O operations in assembly language. For this chapter, we'll focus on a common architecture: x86 assembly using the NASM (Netwide Assembler) syntax, mainly on the Linux operating system, as it offers a rich set of syscalls for I/O operations.

9.2.1 Reading Input

Reading input can be accomplished using system calls that interact with the standard input (stdin). For example, we can use the `sys_read` syscall. Below is an example of reading a string from standard input:

```assembly
section .data
buffer db 256; Buffer to store input buffer_size db 256 ; Maximum input size

section .text global _start
_start:
; syscall: read
mov eax, 3    ; sys_read
mov ebx, 0    ; file descriptor 0 (stdin) mov ecx, buffer
        ; pointer to buffer
mov edx, buffer_size; number of bytes to read


int 0x80      ; call kernel
; Exit the program
mov eax, 1              ; sys_exit xor ebx, ebx    ; return 0
int 0x80      ; call kernel
```

9.2.2 Writing Output

Similar to reading, writing output can also be done via system calls. To write to standard output (stdout), we use the `sys_write` syscall. Here's an example:

```assembly
section .data

message db 'Hello, World!', 0xA ; string to output

section .text global _start

_start:
; syscall: write
mov eax, 4    ; sys_write
mov ebx, 1    ; file descriptor 1 (stdout) mov ecx, message
       ; pointer to the message mov edx, 14          ;
message length
int 0x80    ; call kernel
; Exit the program
mov eax, 1              ; sys_exit xor ebx, ebx    ; return 0
int 0x80    ; call kernel
```

9.2.3 File I/O Operations

File I/O in assembly requires a few more system calls compared to standard input and output. The general steps are to open a file, read or write data, and then close the file. Here is a simple example that demonstrates these operations:

```assembly
section .data

filename db 'example.txt', 0 message db 'Hello, File!', 0xA
buf db 256
```

```
bufsize db 256
section .text global _start
_start:
; Open file
mov eax, 5    ; sys_open
mov ebx, filename  ; pointer to filename

mov ecx, 2              ; O_WRONLY int 0x80    ;        call kernel
mov ebx, eax ; store file descriptor
; Write to file
mov eax, 4    ; sys_write
mov ecx, message   ; pointer to the message mov edx, 14   ; message length
int 0x80      ; call kernel
; Close file
mov eax, 6    ; sys_close
int 0x80      ; call kernel
; Exit the program
mov eax, 1              ; sys_exit xor ebx, ebx    ; return 0
int 0x80    ; call kernel
```

9.3 Error Handling in I/O

When performing I/O operations, it is important to

handle potential errors gracefully. Each system call returns a status code indicating success or failure. A return value of `-1` usually indicates an error. Here's how you might check for errors:

```assembly
; syscall: open mov eax, 5

mov ebx, filename mov ecx, 2

int 0x80 cmp eax, -1

jl error_open; Jump to error handling if file could not be opened
```

By implementing error handling, you can ensure that your program behaves predictably, even under unexpected conditions.

Handling input and output in assembly language can be quite powerful but also requires understanding the details of the underlying architecture and operating system. From basic reading and writing operations to more complex file manipulations, understanding these concepts forms the foundation for building robust assembly programs.

Working with Keyboard Input and Screen Output

This chapter explores the techniques used to manage keyboard input and screen output, covering both basic concepts and practical implementations.

Understanding the Basics of I/O in Assembly

At the core of any assembly program lies the need for the program to communicate with the user. The most common forms of interaction are reading input from the keyboard and displaying text on the screen. These I/O operations are typically handled through system calls or BIOS interrupts, depending on the architecture and environment.

Key Concepts

Assembly Language and Hardware: Assembly language is a low-level programming language that is closely related to the architecture's hardware. This means that handling I/O operations often involves working directly with hardware registers and specific memory addresses.

Interrupts: Interrupts are signals to the processor emitted by hardware or software indicating an event that needs immediate attention. In the context of I/O, interrupts are often used for reading from the keyboard or writing to the screen.

System Calls vs. BIOS Interrupts: Depending on the operating system, there are different methods to perform I/O. For instance, DOS programs frequently rely on BIOS interrupts, while Linux programs might utilize system calls.

Keyboard Input in Assembly Language ### Reading a Character

In x86 assembly, keyboard input can be handled using BIOS interrupt `INT 21h` (in DOS) or `INT 16h`. Here is a simple example to read a character from the keyboard using `INT 16h`:

```asm
section .data
msg db 'Enter a character: ', 0
chr db 0        ; To store the character read
section .text global _start
_start:
; Print message
mov edx, len msg ; Load the message length
mov ecx, msg; Load the address of the message call print_string ; Call function to print string
; Read character
mov ah, 0          ; Function 0: Read character from keyboard int 16h      ; Call BIOS interrupt
mov [chr], al   ; Store the character in \'chr\'
; (Optional) Do something with the character
; ...
; Exit program (Linux syscall or DOS interrupt)
; ...
print_string:
; Function to print a null-terminated string mov eax, 4; Syscall for sys_write in Linux
mov ebx, 1    ; File descriptor for standard output mov ecx, msg            ; Pointer to string
mov edx, 16            ; Length of string int 0x80 ;      Call kernel
ret
```

len:

equ $ - msg   ; Calculate length of msg
```

### Handling Strings

To extend the functionality, we can read an entire string from the keyboard. Again using `INT 21h`, we can set up a buffer and read characters until a newline (Enter key) is pressed.

```asm section .bss

buffer resb 256 ; Allocate space for a buffer

section .text global _start

_start:

; Ask user for input

; ...

; Read string

mov ah, 0Ah ; Function 0Ah: Buffered input lea dx, [buffer] ; Load address of our buffer

int 21h; Call DOS interrupt

; Process input

; ...

; Exit program

; ...
```

Screen Output in Assembly Language ### Displaying Text
```

Assembly language allows you to write directly to the video memory (for DOS) or use system calls for higher-level environments. In DOS, BIOS interrupt `INT 10h` is used for character output.

For instance, to display a single character:

```asm
section .text global _start

_start:

mov ah, 0Eh        ; Function 0Eh: Teletype output mov al, 'A'  ; Character to print

int 10h        ; Call BIOS interrupt

; Exit program

; ...
```

Displaying Strings

To display strings, you may again use BIOS interrupts or write directly to video memory. Here's an example using `INT 10h` to display a string:

```asm
section .data

msg db 'Hello, world!$' ; Strings must end with a dollar sign in DOS

section .text global _start

_start:

; Print string using BIOS interrupt

mov ah, 09h ; Function 09h: Print string with $ terminator lea dx, [msg]  ; Load address of the string

int 10h        ; Call BIOS interrupt
```

; Exit program

; ...

\`\`\`

Working with keyboard input and screen output in assembly programming requires a good understanding of interrupts and system architecture. Through practical examples, we've seen how to handle various types of input and output in both DOS and higher-level OS environments. Mastering these I/O operations is crucial for developing robust interactive applications in assembly language.

Interacting with System Calls and BIOS Interrupts

This chapter focuses on two critical aspects of assembly programming: **system calls** and **BIOS interrupts**. Together, these concepts allow programmers to communicate effectively with the operating system and the hardware, enabling tasks from low-level system manipulations to high-level application interactions.

1. Understanding System Calls ### 1.1 What are System Calls?

A system call is an interface that allows a user program to request services from the operating system's kernel. It acts as a gatekeeper, providing controlled access to hardware resources, file systems, and other critical services. Common examples include reading from or writing to files, creating processes, or managing memory.

1.2 System Call Example

In an x86 environment, a typical way to execute a system call is through specific registers and interrupt instructions. For example, in Linux, the `int 0x80` instruction is commonly used to invoke services. Below is a simple assembly code snippet illustrating how to use system calls to write "Hello, World!" to the console.

```assembly
section .data
hello db 'Hello, World!', 0x0A ; Message with newline

section .text global _start

_start:
; syscall number for sys_write

mov eax, 4    ; syscall number (sys_write) mov ebx, 1   ; file descriptor (stdout) mov ecx, hello         ; pointer to message

mov edx, 14          ; message length int 0x80 ;       call kernel

; Exit the program

mov eax, 1    ; syscall number (sys_exit) xor ebx, ebx   ; exit code 0

int 0x80      ; call kernel
```

1.3 System Call Parameters

Understanding how to pass parameters to system calls is crucial. Parameters are typically passed through registers:

`EAX`: Contains the system call number.

`EBX`: First argument.

132

`ECX`: Second argument.

`EDX`: Third argument.

The above example shows how these registers are employed to execute a write operation. ## 2. BIOS Interrupts

2.1 What are BIOS Interrupts?

BIOS interrupts provide a low-level interface for programs to interact with hardware components on a computer. They are defined in the BIOS and allow routines for disk I/O, keyboard input, and other hardware interactions. BIOS interrupts are mostly used in real mode, typically on x86 architecture before an operating system has fully taken control of the system.

2.2 Using BIOS Interrupts

To use BIOS interrupts, you write to the `AH` register to specify the service you want. Here's an example that demonstrates how to use IRQ 0x10 to display a character on screen:

```assembly
```assembly section .text
global _start

_start:

mov ah, 0x0E          ; BIOS teletype output function
mov al, 'A'    ; Character to print

int 0x10      ; Call BIOS interrupt

; Exit to DOS

mov ax, 0x4C00     ; Terminate program int 0x21
```
```

```

### 2.3 BIOS Interrupt Parameters

When using BIOS interrupts, parameters are typically passed in registers like so:

`AH`: The function number that specifies the service.

`AL`: The character or data to be processed.

Other registers may hold different types of data depending on the function requested. ## 3. Differences and Interactions

### 3.1 System Calls vs. BIOS Interrupts

While both system calls and BIOS interrupts provide functionalities that may overlap, they serve different purposes:

**System Calls**: These are executed under the operating system's control and ensure safety and stability. They handle complex tasks, such as process management and memory allocation.

**BIOS Interrupts**: Operate at a lower level, providing direct access to hardware. They are typically invoked when an operating system has not yet taken control, or in specialized programming contexts, like bootloaders.

### 3.2 Choosing Between BIOS and System Calls

In modern software development, BIOS interrupts are rarely used, given the prevalence of operating systems that provide more sophisticated and safer interfaces via system calls. Nevertheless, understanding BIOS interrupts is essential for systems programming, embedded systems,
```

and for environments where direct hardware control is required.

While system calls offer a more controlled approach through an operating system, BIOS interrupts give you raw access to the hardware, which can be crucial for specific applications. Mastery of these interactions not only enhances your skills in assembly programming but also deepens your understanding of computer architecture and operating system design.

Chapter 10: Understanding and Implementing Interrupts

This chapter delves into the concept of interrupts, their types, handling mechanisms, and practical implementation in assembly programming.

10.1 What are Interrupts?

Interrupts are signals to the processor emitted by hardware or software indicating an event that needs immediate attention. When an interrupt is received, the CPU halts its current task, saves its state, and transfers control to a special routine known as an interrupt handler or interrupt service routine (ISR). After the ISR has executed, control returns to the original process just where it left off.

Types of Interrupts

Hardware Interrupts: Triggered by hardware devices (like timers, I/O devices) to signal events (like data arrival on a port).

Software Interrupts: Generated by programs or the operating system through specific instructions (like system calls).

10.2 Why Use Interrupts?

The use of interrupts provides several advantages:

Responsiveness: The system can respond to asynchronous events (like user input) without polling.

Efficiency: CPU time is saved since the CPU is not constantly checking the status of devices.

Concurrency: Multiple tasks can be handled

effectively, improving multitasking in real-time systems.

10.3 Interrupt Vectors and Handling

When an interrupt occurs, the processor needs to know which ISR to execute. This is managed through the

interrupt vector table (IVT)—a table that contains the addresses of ISRs for various interrupts.

Setting Up the Interrupt Vector Table

Setting the correct addresses for ISRs in the IVT is a fundamental aspect of managing interrupts in assembly.

Example:

For a simple assembly program, let's assume we are using x86 architecture and want to handle a timer interrupt:

```assembly
assembly section .data
; Data section for variables if needed

section .text global _start

_start:

; Set up the interrupt vector for timer interrupt cli     ; Clear interrupts

mov dword [0x20], isr_timer ; Set ISR for IRQ0 (timer interrupt) sti ; Enable interrupts

; Main program loop

.loop:

; Your main code here


jmp .loop     ; Infinite loop for demonstration
```

```
isr_timer:
```

; Your ISR code to handle the timer interrupt

; For example, increment a counter or handle a task iretd
    ; Return from interrupt

```
` ` `
```

Disabling and Enabling Interrupts

In many assembly languages, control over enabling and disabling interrupts is provided. Here is how you typically manage interrupts:

CLI: Clears the interrupt flag (disables interrupts).

STI: Sets the interrupt flag (enables interrupts).

These instructions are crucial in critical sections of code where interrupt handling should not be interrupted further.

10.4 Context Switching

When an interrupt occurs, the CPU needs to save the execution context (registers, program counter) of the currently running process. The saved context allows the CPU to resume its task after completing the ISR.

Context Switch Example

Below is a simplified procedure illustrating how context switching could occur during an interrupt:

```
```assembly isr_timer:
```

pusha ; Push all general-purpose registers onto the stack

; Perform the task needed for the timer interrupt popa ;
Restore registers
```

```
iretd   ; Return from interrupt
```
```

In this example, `pusha` saves the entire register context onto the stack, ensuring that the original process can be restored accurately after addressing the interrupt.

## 10.5 Implementing a Simple Timer Interrupt

To solidify our understanding of interrupts, let's implement a simple timer interrupt that toggles an LED on a hypothetical embedded system. We'll need to configure the timer and write an ISR.

### Configuration Steps:

Configure the timer peripheral to generate interrupts at a regular interval.

Write the ISR to toggle the LED state.

### Example:

```assembly
section .text global _start

_start:
; Configure timer to trigger an interrupt every 100 m s call setup_timer
```

```
; Enable global interrupts sti
.loop:
; Main loop can perform other tasks jmp .loop
setup_timer:
; Logic to set up the timer interrupt (pseudo-code)
```
```

```
; Setting up timer_control_register
; Updating the timer_register for 100ms interval ret
isr_timer:
; Toggle the state of the LED
xor byte [led_state], 1      ; Toggle LED state iretd    ;
Return from interrupt
```
```
```

In this implementation, the ISR performs a simple toggle of an LED state. It assumes that the LED state is stored in memory, represented by `led_state`.

10.6 Debugging Interrupts

Debugging interrupts in assembly programming can be challenging due to their asynchronous nature. Here are some tips for effective debugging:

Use breakpoints sparingly; they can disrupt the timing of your ISR.

Implement logging to a serial port or memory to track interrupt occurrences.

Ensure that the system state before and after the ISR are consistent.

By implementing interrupts properly, you can ensure that your program can handle multiple tasks concurrently and respond quickly to real-time events. As you embark on more complex projects, the principles outlined in this chapter will serve as a solid foundation for the effective use of interrupts in assembly programming.

Software vs. Hardware Interrupts and Their Uses

Interrupts serve as signals that momentarily halt the normal execution of a program, allowing the CPU to address specific conditions or external events. This chapter explores the two primary categories of interrupts: hardware interrupts and software interrupts. We will delve into their characteristics, uses in assembly programming, and how they affect system operation and design.

What are Interrupts?

An interrupt is a signal that indicates to the processor that an event needs immediate attention. When an interrupt occurs, the processor suspends its current activities, saves its state, and executes a special function known as an interrupt service routine (ISR) or interrupt handler. This mechanism allows systems to remain responsive and perform tasks asynchronously.

Types of Interrupts

Interrupts can be broadly categorized into two types: hardware interrupts and software interrupts. ### Hardware Interrupts

Definition

Hardware interrupts are generated by external hardware devices, such as keyboards, mice, disk drives, and network interfaces. These interrupts notify the CPU of events requiring immediate processing. For example, when a user presses a key on the keyboard, a hardware interrupt is issued to signal that a character needs to be read.

Characteristics

Asynchronous: Hardware interrupts can occur at any time, independent of the program flow.

High Priority: Many hardware interrupts are assigned a higher priority to ensure time-sensitive processing.

Interrupt Vector Table (IVT): The CPU maintains an IVT that maps interrupt requests to their corresponding ISR addresses, facilitating quick context switching.

Use Cases

Hardware interrupts are commonly used in scenarios such as:

I/O Operations: When a device has completed a task (e.g., a disk read), it raises an interrupt, prompting the processor to retrieve the data.

Real-Time Processing: In real-time systems, hardware interrupts are used to manage timing and trigger immediate task execution.

Software Interrupts #### Definition

Software interrupts, also known as exceptions or traps, are generated by programs due to specific conditions,

such as division by zero, invalid memory access, or system calls. They are intentionally triggered by a program to communicate with the operating system or to handle errors gracefully.

Characteristics

Synchronous: Software interrupts occur in direct response to executing code and typically cause the CPU to transition into a different execution state.

Easily Controllable: Developers can strategically place software interrupts to manage specific exceptions or invoke system services.

Defined Behavior: Each software interrupt is associated with particular conditions or services defined by the system, ensuring controlled execution.

Use Cases

Software interrupts are useful for:

Error Handling: Capturing exceptions and taking necessary actions, such as logging errors or displaying messages to users.

System Calls: Enabling user programs to request services from the operating system, like file operations or memory allocation.

Assembly Programming and Interrupts

Assembly language is a low-level programming language closely aligned with the architecture of computer hardware. Handling interrupts in assembly programming requires an understanding of the specific CPU architecture and its assembly language syntax.

Using Hardware Interrupts in Assembly

Hardware interrupts are typically managed through the following steps:

Enable Interrupts: The processor's interrupt flag must be set to allow handling of hardware interrupts.

Define ISRs: Programmers write interrupt service routines that will execute when a specific hardware interrupt occurs. These routines must save the CPU state and perform the required tasks.

Register ISRs: The addresses of the ISRs are registered in the interrupt vector table.

Handle Interrupts: When an interrupt occurs, the CPU will automatically jump to the ISR defined for the corresponding interrupt.

Below is a simplified assembly code snippet illustrating a hardware interrupt setup:

```assembly
```assembly section .text global _start

_start:
; Set up the interrupt vector table
; Assuming interrupt number for keyboard is 0x21
; Load ISR address
mov [0x21*4], isr_keyboard
; Enable interrupts sti
; Main loop
.loop:
; Do something jmp .loop
isr_keyboard:
; Handle keyboard interrupt
; Read key from keyboard port

; Send End-of-Interrupt signal
; Acknowledge the interrupt
```
```

```
iret
```

Using Software Interrupts in Assembly

Software interrupts are invoked using specific assembly instructions, allowing the program to transition into an interrupt handler. In x86 architecture, for example, the `INT` instruction is commonly used.

Here's a code example using a software interrupt for a simple system call:

```assembly
section .text global _start

_start:
; Prepare parameters for the system call
; For example, calling for a write operation
mov eax, 1     ; syscall number for sys_write mov ebx, 1; file descriptor (1 = stdout) mov ecx, msg          ; pointer to the message mov edx, msg_len          ; length of the message
int 0x80       ; invoke the kernel
; Exit the program
mov eax, 1     ; syscall number for sys_exit xor ebx, ebx; return 0
int 0x80
section .data
msg db 'Hello, World!', 0 msg_len equ $ - msg
```

Understanding the distinction between hardware and software interrupts is fundamental for assembly programming and system design. Hardware interrupts provide the mechanism for efficient real-time operations and event handling, while software interrupts offer a controlled means to manage exceptional conditions and invoke system services.

Using Interrupts for System-Level Operations

This chapter will delve into the fundamentals of interrupts, their types, how they are implemented in assembly language, and practical applications that demonstrate their utility in system-level operations.

Understanding Interrupts

An interrupt is a signal to the processor emitted by hardware or software indicating an event that needs immediate attention. Interrupts allow the CPU to stop executing the current sequence of instructions and execute a special routine, known as an interrupt service routine (ISR). After the ISR completes its task, control is returned to the original program.

Types of Interrupts

Interrupts can be categorized into several types:

Hardware Interrupts: These are generated by hardware devices (like keyboards, mice, or network cards) to signal events. For instance, when a key is pressed, the keyboard controller sends a hardware interrupt to the CPU.

Software Interrupts: These interrupts can be

generated by software instructions. In assembly language, this is often done using an `INT` instruction followed by a specific interrupt number (vector) that indicates the operation required.

Timer Interrupts: These are a specific type of hardware interrupts that are generated by a system timer. They are crucial for multitasking operating systems as they provide a way to switch between different processes.

Exceptions: These interrupts occur as a result of errors or special conditions in the execution of a program, such as division by zero or invalid memory access.

How Interrupts Work

When an interrupt is triggered, the processor suspends its current task and saves the state of its registers, program counter, and other critical information. It then uses the interrupt vector (a predefined memory address that denotes the ISR associated with that interrupt) to jump to the appropriate ISR.

An ISR must be efficient and short-lived because it temporarily halts the main program. Once the ISR finishes executing, the saved state is restored, and the CPU resumes its previous work.

Implementing Interrupts in Assembly Language

To work with interrupts in assembly language, a programmer typically follows these steps:

Define the ISR: This is a special routine that will handle a specific interrupt.

Set Up the Interrupt Vector Table: This table associates each interrupt number with its ISR address.

Enable Interrupts: The processor must be instructed to react to interrupt requests. ### Example: Setting Up a Simple Timer Interrupt

Here's an example to illustrate how a simple timer interrupt could be set up and handled in assembly language. The following is a hypothetical implementation using x86 architecture (real mode), which outlines the steps involved.

```assembly section .text global _start

_start:

; Set up the interrupt service routine (ISR) cli   ;   Clear interrupts

; Calculate ISR address; assume it's at 'timer_isr' label address lea ax, [timer_isr]

mov [0x20 * 4], ax  ; Set up IRQ0 for timer interrupt (vector 32) sti    ; Set interrupts on

; Main loop main_loop:

hlt    ; Halt CPU until next interrupt jmp main_loop    ; Infinite loop

; Define the Timer Interrupt Service Routine timer_isr:

; Acknowledge the interrupt (specific to the hardware)

; For x86, we send an EOI (End Of Interrupt) signal to PIC mov al, 0x20 ; Command to PIC to acknowledge

out 0x20, al

; Do some work, e.g., updating a system tick counter

; Return from interrupt
```

```
iret    ; Return to interrupted program
```
```
`  `  `
```

Explanation of the Code

Setting Up the ISR: The ISR `timer_isr` is defined at the end of the code.

CLI/STI Instructions: The `cli` instruction disables interrupts to avoid nesting interrupts while setting up the ISR. The `sti` instruction enables interrupts, allowing the processor to respond to them.

Acknowledge the Interrupt: The ISR starts by sending an EOI signal on the appropriate port to let the PIC (Programmable Interrupt Controller) know that the interrupt has been serviced.

Return from Interrupt: The `iret` instruction is essential as it restores the state of the registers and allows the CPU to continue executing the main program from where it was interrupted.

Practical Applications of Interrupts

Using interrupts for system-level operations has numerous applications, including:

Real-time Processing: In scenarios where real-time processing is critical (e.g., robotics, embedded systems), interrupts allow immediate response to events.

Multitasking: Operating systems use timer interrupts to implement scheduling, allowing multiple processes to share the CPU effectively.

Event-driven Programming: GUI applications can benefit greatly from interrupts, allowing the system to respond to user inputs (like mouse clicks) asynchronously.

Peripheral Management: Hardware devices can signal the CPU when they are ready for communication (like I/O devices), allowing efficient data processing without the need for constant polling.

Understanding and utilizing interrupts is fundamental for effective assembly programming, particularly in system-level operations. They provide a means for the system to respond promptly to events, manage multiple tasks, and interact with hardware efficiently.

Chapter 11: Assembly Language and File Handling

While high-level languages abstract away the complexities of hardware management, assembly language provides the granularity needed to manipulate hardware directly. In this chapter, we explore the fundamental concepts of assembly language, its syntax, the instructions used for various operations, and its application in file handling.

1. Understanding Assembly Language ### 1.1 The Purpose of Assembly Language

Assembly language allows programmers to write low-level code that can be efficiently executed by the CPU. Each assembly language instruction corresponds to a specific machine instruction for a given architecture, making it easier to utilize system resources. This language is hardware-specific, meaning that assembly code written for one type of CPU (e.g., x86) may not work on another (e.g., ARM).

1.2 Structure of Assembly Language

An assembly language program is composed of several components:

Mnemonics: Human-readable representations of machine instructions (e.g., `MOV`, `ADD`, `SUB`).

Operands: The variables or constant values that instructions operate on.

Directives: Instructions to the assembler itself that guide the assembly process (e.g., `.data`, `.text`).

Labels: Named markers that denote locations in the

code, often used for jump instructions. ### 1.3 Basic Syntax

An assembly program typically starts with the definition of the data segment followed by the code segment:

```asm
section .data
```

msg db 'Hello, World!', 0 ; Null-terminated string

section .text global _start

_start:

; Code to print message

; ...
```
```

In this example, the `.data` section defines a string variable `msg`, and the `.text` section contains the executable code.

2. Assembly Language Operations ### 2.1 Arithmetic Operations

Assembly language provides several instructions for performing arithmetic operations. These operations, like addition and subtraction, usually involve registers:

```asm
```

MOV AX, 5   ; Load 5 into register AX ADD AX, 3
          ; Add 3 to the value in AX
```
```

2.2 Logical Operations

Logical operations such as AND, OR, and NOT are also common in assembly programming. They manipulate the individual bits of operand values.

```asm
MOV AL, 0b10101010 ; Load binary value into AL

AND AL, 0b11110000  ; Perform bitwise AND with another binary value
```

2.3 Control Flow

Control flow is managed using jump instructions that alter the sequential execution of instructions based on conditions:

```asm
CMP AX, BX ; Compare AX to BX

JE equal_label ; Jump to equal_label if they are equal
```

3. File Handling in Assembly Language

File handling in assembly language is a lower-level operation typically done through system calls. The methods to interact with files differ between operating systems, but let's explore file handling in a Linux environment using system calls.

3.1 Opening a File

To open a file, the `open` system call is used:

```asm
section .data

filename db 'example.txt', 0 ; File name with null terminator flags db 0        ; No special flags

section .text global _start
```

153

```asm
_start:
; Open the file
mov rax, 2     ; syscall number for open lea rdi, [filename]
               ; filename pointer
mov rsi, 0     ; flags - read only syscall
```

3.2 Reading from a File

Once the file is opened, you can read from it using the `read` system call:

```asm
section .bss
buffer resb 128        ; Allocate a buffer for reading
section .text
; Assuming the file descriptor is stored in rax
mov rax, 0     ; syscall number for read
mov rdi, rax   ; file descriptor
lea rsi, [buffer]      ; buffer pointer
mov rdx, 128 ; bytes to read syscall
```

3.3 Writing to a File

To write data to a file, the `write` system call is employed:

```asm
section .text
mov rax, 1     ; syscall number for write
mov rdi, rax   ; file descriptor, same as for read
lea rsi, [buffer]      ; data to write
```

154

mov rdx, 128 ; bytes to write syscall

` ` `

3.4 Closing a File

Finally, it is crucial to close a file after operations are completed using the `close` system call:

` ` `asm

mov rax, 3   ; syscall number for close

mov rdi, rax ; file descriptor syscall

` ` `

We explored assembly language as a powerful tool for low-level programming and file handling. Understanding how to manipulate data and control flow in assembly allows developers more direct and efficient resource management. While file handling in assembly language is significantly more complex than in high-level languages, it provides an invaluable insight into the underlying processes that constitute computer operations.

Reading and Writing Files in Assembly

This chapter delves into the intricacies of reading from and writing to files using assembly language, exploring how to manipulate file handles and perform operations using both DOS and Linux system calls.

Understanding File Operations in Assembly

Before diving into coding, it is essential to comprehend the fundamental concepts of file operations. Files are represented by file handles, which are essentially integer identifiers that the operating system uses to manage access to the file. Common operations for file handling include:

Opening a file

Reading from a file

Writing to a file

Closing a file

These operations differ slightly depending on the operating system and the architecture you are working with. In this chapter, we will focus on examples for both DOS (using INT 21h) and Linux (using syscall).

File I/O in DOS ### Opening a File

In DOS, we often work with the BIOS interrupt `INT 21h` to perform file I/O operations. To open a file, we use the `function 3Dh` service:

```assembly
section .data

filename db 'example.txt', 0  ; Null-terminated string for
the filename filehandle dw 0      ; To store the file handle

section .text global _start


_start:
```

```asm
; Open the file with read/write access mov ah, 3Dh
mov al, 0      ; Open for reading
lea dx, [filename]          ; Load filename address int 21h
       ; Call DOS interrupt
jc error       ; Jump if there was an error mov
[filehandle], ax           ; Store the file handle
; Error handling can be implemented here
```

Reading from a File

Once a file is opened, we can read its contents. This is done using the `function 3Fh`. Here's how you can read from the file into a buffer:

```asm
assembly section .bss

buffer resb 128  ; Allocate 128 bytes for reading

section .text

; Assume the file is already opened

read_file:

mov ah, 3Fh           ; Function to read from file mov bx,
[filehandle] ; Load the file handle lea dx, [buffer]      ;
Buffer to store data

mov cx, 128           ; Number of bytes to read int 21h  ;
Call DOS interrupt

jc error       ; Jump if there was an error

; Proceed to use the data in buffer
```

Writing to a File

To write data to the file, we can make use of `function 40h`. Here's a simple example:

```assembly
section .data
data_to_write db 'Hello, World!', 0
data_length equ $ - data_to_write  ; Length of the data
write_file:
mov ah, 40h  ; Function to write to file mov bx, [filehandle] ; Load the file handle lea dx, [data_to_write] ; Data to write
mov cx, data_length  ; Length of the data to write int 21h      ; Call DOS interrupt
jc error        ; Jump if there was an error
```

Closing a File

Finally, it is crucial to close the file after operations are completed. This can be achieved using `function 3Eh`:

```assembly
close_file:
mov ah, 3Eh        ; Function to close a file mov bx, [filehandle] ; Load the file handle int 21h        ; Call DOS interrupt
```

File I/O in Linux

Linux interacts with files through system calls. This section will guide you through the process of reading from and writing to files using the syscall interface.

158

Opening a File

In Linux, you typically use the `sys_open` syscall. Here's how you can open a file:

```assembly
section .data

filename db 'example.txt', 0 file_flags db 0  ; O_RDONLY

section .bss filehandle resb 4

section .text global _start

_start:

; Open the file

mov eax, 5   ; syscall number for sys_open lea ebx, [filename] ; pointer to filename

mov ecx, 0          ; O_RDONLY int 0x80   ;   Call kernel

mov [filehandle], eax ; Store the file handle
```

Reading from a File

To read data from a file in Linux, you can use the `sys_read` syscall:

```assembly
section .bss

buffer resb 128  ; Buffer to hold read data

bytes_read resb 4 ; To store the number of bytes read

section .text read_file:

mov eax, 3   ; syscall number for sys_read mov ebx, [filehandle] ; File handle

lea ecx, [buffer] ; Buffer
```

```
mov edx, 128        ; Number of bytes to read int 0x80
    ; Call kernel
mov [bytes_read], eax ; Store the number of bytes read
```
```

### Writing to a File

To write data, you can use the `sys_write` syscall:

```
```assembly section .data
data_to_write db 'Hello, World!', 0
write_file:
mov eax, 4   ; syscall number for sys_write mov ebx, [filehandle] ; File handle
lea ecx, [data_to_write] ; Address of the data to write mov edx, 13        ; Number of bytes to write int 0x80        ; Call kernel
```
```

### Closing a File

After completing all read and write operations, it is vital to close the file:

```
```assembly close_file:
mov eax, 6   ; syscall number for sys_close mov ebx, [filehandle] ; File handle
int 0x80     ; Call kernel
```
```

Mastering file I/O in assembly can be challenging but rewarding, as it introduces you to the low-level workings of file management in a computer system. Whether you
```

are working in DOS or Linux, understanding the methods and system calls used for opening, reading, writing, and closing files is fundamental in becoming proficient in assembly programming.

4. Closing the File

Finally, it is crucial to close any file descriptors when they are no longer needed to free up resources:

```assembly
; Close the file descriptor

mov rax, 3     ; syscall number for close (sys_close) syscall
```

Error Handling

In real-world applications, error handling is paramount. After each system call, checking the return value can help identify whether the operation was successful (usually a non-negative number) or failed (a negative number). This requires implementing branches based on the success of these calls, and appropriate error handling routines should be part of any practical assembly program.

By using system calls to interface with the operating system, programmers can manage files efficiently, enabling powerful manipulations that are the backbone of many applications. As you become more proficient in assembly language, mastering these concepts will aid you in developing robust systems-level software.

Chapter 12: Debugging and Troubleshooting Assembly Code

This chapter offers a comprehensive guide on debugging and troubleshooting assembly code, including techniques, tools, and best practices to expedite the process and improve code quality.

12.1 Understanding Common Pitfalls

Before diving into debugging techniques, it is essential to be aware of common pitfalls associated with assembly language programming. Many of these stem from the complexity and specificity of the language, such as:

12.1.1 Syntax Errors

Due to the rigid syntax of assembly language, even minor deviations can lead to syntax errors. Always ensure proper formatting, and pay attention to the following:

Missing colons and brackets

Incorrect use of directives

Misspelled instructions or operands ### 12.1.2 Register Mismanagement

Registers are the CPU's way of storing temporary data, and improper handling can result in unpredictable behavior. Common issues include:

Overwriting register values without saving previous data

Using the wrong register for operations

Forgetting to clear flags or status registers before use ### 12.1.3 Memory Access Violations

Improper management of memory addresses leads to

segmentation faults or accessing incorrect memory locations. It's crucial to:

Ensure pointer arithmetic is correct.

Maintain bounds checking to prevent overflow.

Utilize proper data segment directives for global and local variables. ### 12.1.4 Control Flow Missteps

Managing control flow can be tricky in assembly due to jumps and branches. Bugs often emerge from:

Incorrectly programmed jump instructions (e.g., JNE, JZ).

Infinite loops resulting from incorrect loop conditions.

Not accounting for the state of flags before branching. ## 12.2 Tools and Techniques for Debugging

Having established common pitfalls, we can now explore the tools and techniques available for debugging assembly code effectively.

12.2.1 Assembler Output

When compiling assembly code, most assemblers generate additional output files—be it object files, listing files, or symbol tables. By examining these outputs, you can:

Check for unresolved symbols and dependencies.

See the generated machine code for a better understanding of instruction translations. ### 12.2.2 Debuggers

Debuggers are invaluable for diagnosing and rectifying issues in assembly code. Tools such as GDB (GNU Debugger) allow step-by-step execution, inspecting registers, memory, and operational flow. Here are some functionalities to leverage:

Breakpoints: Pause execution at specific points to examine the state of the program.

Watchpoints: Monitor specific memory locations, triggering alerts when values change.

Step Over/Step Into: Execute instructions line-by-line to track behavior closely, especially across function calls.

12.2.3 Emulators and Simulators

Using emulators or simulators can simplify the debugging process. These tools mimic the CPU environment and allow for:

Applying instruction tracing to see the effect of each instruction on the state of the machine.

Simulating hardware interactions, providing insight into peripheral behavior. ### 12.2.4 Logging and Tracing

Incorporating logging statements into your assembly program can be a useful strategy. By outputting register values and flow control points to the console, you can track:

The sequence of executed instructions.

The state of key variables or registers.

Points of failure in the logic flow.

12.3 Best Practices for Assembly Programming

To minimize debugging time and improve code maintainability, consider adopting the following best practices:

12.3.1 Comment Extensively

Assembly code can be difficult to read, especially for intricate logic. Use comments liberally to explain the purpose of sections of code, the function of registers, and the meaning of parameters. This not only assists debugging but also benefits future maintainers or collaborators.

12.3.2 Modular Programming

Breaking down large programs into smaller, manageable functions or modules can simplify both debugging and testing. This also facilitates easier reuse of code and a clearer understanding of the relationships between components.

12.3.3 Utilize Assertions

Incorporate assertions in your code, which can validate expected states during runtime. This can help catch logical errors early and prevent further complications.

12.3.4 Review and Refactor

Regularly review and refactor your code to maintain clarity and optimize performance. Often, small corrections or refinements can eliminate bugs before they become problematic.

12.4 Case Studies

12.4.1 Case Study 1: Fixing a Loop Condition

Consider an assembly routine meant to compute the sum of integers from 1 to N. A bug manifested through an infinite loop due to a miscalculated condition. During debugging with GDB, a breakpoint was placed before the loop to assess the loop variable. By tracing the instruction that decremented the loop counter, the programmer discovered that they mistakenly compared an unsigned integer against a signed one.

In another scenario, a memory access violation emerged during a string manipulation function. The programmer leveraged an emulator to visualize memory operations. By stepping through each instruction, they identified off-by-one errors in memory access, leading to adjustments that resolved segmentation faults.

Debugging isn't merely a corrective measure—it's an essential skill that sharpens your programming expertise and deepens your understanding of computers' inner workings.

Using Debugging Tools Like GDB and OllyDbg

Unlike higher-level languages that often abstract away the intricacies of memory management and execution flow, Assembly programming exposes developers to the nitty-gritty details, making effective debugging even more essential. This chapter will explore how to use two powerful debugging tools: GDB (GNU Debugger) and OllyDbg, to streamline the debugging process in assembly programming.

1. Introduction to Debugging in Assembly Language

Debugging is the process of identifying and resolving bugs or defects in software. In Assembly language, where the correspondence between code statements and machine instructions is direct, understanding how to trace through your code is paramount. Common issues in assembly programming may include incorrect memory access, miscalculated addresses, or logical errors due to the

166

complexity of managing registers and low-level constructs.

2. Getting Started with GDB

GDB, the GNU Debugger, is a powerful command-line debugging tool widely used for debugging applications written in C, C++, and Assembly. To begin using GDB for assembly programs, the following steps should be followed:

2.1 Setting Up the Environment

Install GDB: Ensure you have GDB installed on your system. On Debian-based systems, you can use

`sudo apt-get install gdb`.

Compile with Debug Symbols: When compiling your assembly code, use the `-g` flag with your assembler (for example, `nasm` or `gcc`) to include debug symbols. This allows GDB to access source-level information.

```bash
nasm -g -f elf64 your_program.asm gcc -o your_program your_program.o
```

2.2 Basic GDB Commands

Once you have GDB running with your assembly program, you can utilize several key commands:

`run (r)`: Starts the execution of your program.

`break (b)`: Sets a breakpoint at a given line or function, allowing you to pause execution.

```bash
(gdb) break main
```

`next (n)`: Executes the next line of code, stepping over function calls.

`step (s)`: Executes the next line, stepping into function calls.

`print (p)`: Displays the value of a variable or register.

```bash

(gdb) print $eax  ; Example for displaying the value in the EAX register.
```

`continue (c)`: Resumes execution after hitting a breakpoint. ### 2.3 Analyzing Execution Flow

One of the primary use cases for GDB is to analyze the execution flow. Using breakpoints, you can pause execution at strategic locations and inspect registers, memory, and the stack. This enables you to determine if your code executes as expected and helps identify logical errors.

2.4 Inspecting Memory and Registers

In assembly language programming, keeping track of registers and memory is critical. Use commands like

`info registers` to get the values of all CPU registers and

`x` to examine memory.

```bash
(gdb) info registers

(gdb) x/16xw $esp  ; Examine 16 words in hexadecimal
starting from the address in ESP.
```

3. Debugging with OllyDbg

OllyDbg is a 32-bit assembler level analyzing debugger for Windows, which is particularly user-friendly for those working with Windows applications written in Assembly.

3.1 Installation and Setup

Download and Install: Get the latest version of OllyDbg from its official website and extract the files.

Open your Executable: Launch OllyDbg, and open the executable you want to debug. OllyDbg will disassemble the executable and display it in an intuitive user interface.

3.2 Navigating the OllyDbg Interface

Familiarize yourself with the OllyDbg interface, which includes:

The **Disassembly View**: Here you can see the assembly code, with spaces for navigating different segments of the code.

The **Registers View**: Displays CPU registers and their current values.

The **Stack View**: Shows the current call stack and local variables. ### 3.3 Setting Breakpoints and Analyzing Code

Like GDB, OllyDbg allows you to set breakpoints by double-clicking on a line of code. Use the following actions to analyze the execution:

Run (F9): Resume execution of the program until the next breakpoint.

Step Over (F8): Execute the next instruction but does not go inside functions.

Step Into (F7): Execute the next instruction and enters functions. ### 3.4 Using the Memory Window

You can activate the memory window to observe and manipulate memory at runtime. This can be critical for determining buffer overflows or incorrect memory management, which are frequent issues in assembly programs.

4. Best Practices for Debugging Assembly Code

To effectively debug assembly programs, consider the following best practices:

Annotate Your Code: Commenting your assembly instructions helps both during debugging and future revisions.

Break Down Complex Sections: If facing difficulties understanding a segment, try to isolate and test smaller pieces through separate subroutines.

Use Logging: Consider implementing logging actions within your code to print variable values and execution points to assist with debugging your logic.

Familiarize Yourself with System Calls: Understand how to use system calls for your operating system to handle input/output, as this knowledge is key during debugging.

Debugging assembly programs can seem daunting due to the intricacies involved. However, by leveraging tools like GDB and OllyDbg, you can effectively manage and troubleshoot your code. Mastering these tools not only boosts your productivity but also enhances your understanding of how assembly programs operate at a fundamental level.

Common Assembly Errors and How to Fix Them

In this chapter, we will explore some of the most common assembly errors, their causes, and practical solutions to resolve them.

Understanding Assembly Language Errors

Assembly language programming requires a meticulous approach, as even minor mistakes can lead to significant issues such as program crashes, incorrect outputs, or undefined behavior. Unlike high-level programming languages, assembly lacks built-in error checking mechanisms, making it essential for developers to be vigilant. Here, we will categorize common errors into three main types: syntax errors, logical errors, and runtime errors.

1. Syntax Errors #### Common Issues:

Syntax errors occur when the code deviates from the rules of assembly language. These can include

misspellings, incorrect operation formats, or improper use of directives.

Examples:

Missing a colon (`:`) after a label.

Incorrect formatting of an instruction (e.g., using `MOV A, B` instead of `MOV Ax, Bx` in x86 assembly).

Typos in mnemonics or operands.

How to Fix:

Check the Syntax: Refer to your assembler's documentation for the correct syntax structure.

Use an Assembler with Error Reporting: Many assemblers provide detailed error messages that can pinpoint the line and nature of the error, making it easier to identify and correct.

Code Formatting: Maintain consistent formatting and indentation to improve readability and catch typos more easily.

2. Logical Errors #### Common Issues:

Logical errors occur when the code compiles successfully but does not function as intended. These often stem from miscalculated branch conditions, incorrect register usage, or flawed algorithm implementation.

Examples:

An infinite loop due to improper loop termination conditions.

Errors in arithmetic operations caused by incorrect register manipulation.

Branch instructions that lead to unintended code paths.

How to Fix:

Step through the Code: Utilize debugging tools that

allow for step-by-step execution to monitor the flow of the program and inspect register values at each stage.

Implement Testing Procedures: Break your code into smaller sections and test each part individually to isolate the source of the logical error.

Review Algorithm: Revisit the algorithm to ensure it is implemented correctly in assembly. Documenting the logic outside of code can clarify your understanding and reveal flaws.

3. Runtime Errors

Common Issues:

Runtime errors are exceptions that occur while the program is executing. This can result from accessing invalid memory addresses, stack overflows, or incorrect interactions with system calls.

Examples:

Attempting to divide by zero, which leads to exceptions.

Dereferencing a null pointer or an uninitialized register.

Buffer overflows in string manipulations.

How to Fix:

Input Validation: Always validate input values before performing operations, especially those that can result in runtime exceptions.

Memory Management: Ensure memory allocations are correct and that you are not exceeding defined bounds.

Debugging and Logging: Incorporate logging throughout your code to capture the state and flow prior to runtime errors. Analyze logs to pinpoint the exact locations of failures.

Additional Tips for Error Prevention

Comment Generously: Document your code liberally to provide context for users who follow your logic and to help you remember your thinking during the coding phase.

Utilize Development Tools: Use Integrated Development Environments (IDEs) or tools that support assembly language, offering debugging, syntax highlighting, and error detection features.

Study Example Code: Analyze working assembly code from reputable sources to familiarize yourself with correct practices. Understanding well-written code can help you avoid common pitfalls.

Practice Regularly: Like any skill, regular practice will enhance your proficiency in identifying and rectifying assembly errors. Solve coding challenges and work on varied projects to expand your knowledge base.

By following best practices, utilizing debugging tools, and maintaining a keen attention to detail, you can effectively reduce the incidence of errors in your assembly code and create efficient, functional programs.

Conclusion

As we reach the end of our journey through the intricacies of assembly programming, we reflect on the empowering knowledge you've gained throughout this book. Assembly language serves as a powerful bridge between high-level

174

programming and the hardware that executes your commands, granting you unprecedented control over computer systems.

We started by demystifying the role of assembly in modern computing, discussing its relevance even in an era dominated by high-level languages. You learned about the architecture of computer systems, the fundamentals of binary mathematics, and how these concepts lay the groundwork for understanding assembly.

Through practical examples and exercises, we delved into the core principles of assembly programming, exploring syntax, instruction sets, and how to manipulate data at the lowest level. You've developed skills to interact with memory, utilize registers effectively, and implement algorithms that translate directly into machine code.

As you close this book, remember that mastering assembly programming is not just about writing code; it's about gaining a deeper appreciation of how computers operate. This knowledge will serve you in various ways, enhancing your problem-solving abilities and significantly improving your programming proficiency in higher-level languages.

We encourage you to keep experimenting and building upon the skills you've acquired. The world of assembly programming is vast, filled with opportunities for further exploration in systems programming, embedded systems, or even creating your own operating systems. Continue to seek challenges, and don't hesitate to dive into projects that push your understanding further.

Thank you for embarking on this educational adventure with us. As you move forward, we hope you carry the spirit of curiosity and innovation that assembly programming demands. With your newfound skills, you're now equipped to tackle complex programming tasks and interact with hardware like never before. Happy coding!

Biography

Louis Madson is a passionate innovator and expert in the world of **Madson**, dedicated to sharing knowledge and empowering others through his writing. With a deep understanding of the subject and years of hands-on experience, Louis has become a trusted voice, guiding readers toward mastery with clarity and precision.

Beyond his expertise in **Madson**, Louis is an avid enthusiast of **Assembly programming language**, drawn to its raw power and intricate logic. His fascination with low-level computing fuels his relentless pursuit of knowledge, always pushing the boundaries of what's possible.

When he's not immersed in his craft, Louis enjoys exploring new technologies, solving complex coding puzzles, and inspiring others to embrace the art of problem-solving. His writing is more than just information—it's a **journey of discovery**, designed to ignite curiosity and empower readers to take action.

Through his eBook, Louis Madson invites you to dive deep into **Madson**, equipping you with the tools, insights, and inspiration to turn knowledge into expertise.

Glossary: Assembly Programming for Beginners

A

Addressing Mode

The method used to access data in memory. Different addressing modes, such as immediate, direct, indirect, and register, provide various ways to specify operands for instructions.

Assembler

A tool or program that translates assembly language code into machine code, which can be executed by a computer's CPU. The assembler performs the vital job of transforming human-readable instructions into a language that the computer can understand.

--- ## B

Binary

A numerical system that uses only two digits, 0 and 1. In assembly programming, data and instructions are often expressed in binary form, which is the fundamental language of computers.

--- ## C

Control Flow

Refers to the order in which individual statements, instructions, or function calls are executed or evaluated in a program. Control flow is managed with branch instructions, loops, and function calls in assembly language.

Compiler

Though primarily associated with high-level languages, a compiler may generate inline assembly code as a part of the optimization process or to provide low-level access to system hardware.

CPU (Central Processing Unit)

The main part of a computer that performs most of the processing. The CPU executes machine code instructions and directly interacts with memory and input/output devices.

--- ## D

Directive

Commands in assembly language that provide instructions to the assembler but do not result in machine code. Directives might include data definition, memory allocation, and other non-executable instructions.

Data Segment

A section of memory used to store variables, constants, and data structures. In assembly language, the data segment is where the program's data is defined and accessed.

E

Entry Point

The specific location in the program where execution begins. In assembly, the entry point might be designated by a specific label, typically defined in the source code.

--- ## G

Global Variable

A variable that can be accessed from any part of the

program. In assembly, global variables are often defined using specific directives that allocate space in memory.

--- ## I

Immediate Value

A constant value hard coded directly into the instruction. This value is used as an operand in the operation and is not stored in memory.

Instruction Set Architecture (ISA)

The abstract model of a computer that defines the supported instructions, registers, memory structure, and any accessible hardware features. Different CPUs have different ISAs, which determine the assembly language syntax and capabilities.

--- ## L

Label

A symbolic name that represents a memory address in assembly code. Labels are used to mark specific instructions or data locations for reference, especially in branch and jump instructions.

Low-Level Language

Programming languages that provide little abstraction from a computer's instruction set architecture. Assembly language is a type of low-level language that allows for direct manipulation of hardware resources.

--- ## M

Machine Code

The binary representation of instructions that a CPU can

execute directly. Machine code is generated by the assembler from assembly language and is specific to the architecture of the CPU.

Macro

A sequence of instructions grouped under a single name that can be reused throughout the assembly code. Macros help reduce redundancy and simplify complex sequences of instructions.

--- ## O

Operand

The part of an instruction that specifies the data or the address of the data to be acted upon. Each assembly instruction may include one or more operands.

--- ## P

Prologue

The section of a function or procedure in assembly programming that sets up the environment for execution. It typically involves saving register states and allocating space on the stack.

Push and Pop

Instructions used to add (push) or remove (pop) data from the stack. Pushing a value onto the stack places it on top, while popping retrieves the top value.

--- ## R

Register

A small amount of storage available in the CPU for high-speed data processing. Registers hold temporary data and are integral to the execution of instructions.

Runtime

The period during which a program is executing. Understanding how assembly code behaves at runtime can greatly enhance debugging and optimization efforts.

--- ## S

Stack

A data structure used for storing temporary data, where the last item added is the first to be removed (LIFO – Last In, First Out). The stack is crucial in managing function calls and local variables.

Subroutine

A set of instructions that perform a specific task, which can be called from multiple places within a program. Subroutines help modularize code and improve readability.